ALL ABOUT
TIME

Written by Mari Holloway

**NURSERY
WORLD**

TES
THE TIMES EDUCATIONAL SUPPLEMENT

NURSERY WORLD

TES
THE TIMES EDUCATIONAL SUPPLEMENT

Managing Editor Patricia Grogan
Art Editor Nicola Liddiard

Photography Andy Crawford

Editor Samantha Gray
Editorial assistant Edward FitzGerald
Consultant Marian Whitehead

First published in Great Britain in 1999 by
Times Supplements Limited
Admiral House, 66–68 East Smithfield, London E1 9XY

A CIP catalogue record for this book is available
from the British Library

ISBN 1-84122-004-3

Colour reproduction by Prima Creative Services, UK
Printed and bound in Belgium by Proost

Nursery World would like to thank the children and
staff at the following Kidsunlimited nurseries for
taking part in this book:
Mango Tree Nursery, London and
Toddlers Inn Nursery, London

CONTENTS

INTRODUCTION

All About Time contains more than 100 activities divided into seven chapters. Each chapter explores one avenue of the book's central theme. The activities are self-contained but also build from each other, so you can either dip into several chapters when planning your theme or you can use complete chapters. All the activities are firmly underpinned by seven areas of learning to help you incorporate them into your planning. The topic web on pages 10–11 shows you into which areas of learning each activity falls and each activity has symbols representing the areas of learning covered.

Planning a curriculum

The activities in this book are suitable for curriculum planning following all the early-years guidelines across the United Kingdom. It is widely accepted that young children learn most effectively through first-hand experiences presented through investigative, sensory, imaginative, creative and constructive, play-based activities. Children should be given opportunities to observe, represent, recall, describe, and question. This book gives many ideas for developing these skills, although it should not be seen as providing a complete curriculum. The book's main purpose is to help you build a balanced, varied and interesting curriculum for children of nursery age when presenting aspects of the complex theme of Time. Each activity covers one or more of the following areas of learning: Personal and Social Development, Language and Literacy, Mathematics, Science and Technology, Time and Place, Physical Development, Creative Development.

Personal and Social Development

This is a key area of the nursery curriculum as it incorporates all aspects of children's personal, moral, social and spiritual development. It is at this stage that children are learning to function in groups beyond the family, hence it is essential to provide a safe, stimulating and supportive environment, as well as to recognise the need to encourage independence and to provide challenge where possible. Children are learning how to cooperate with others, sharing resources and taking fair turns, and developing their ability to form relationships. They are beginning to develop an awareness of, and respect for, cultural, religious and social differences, and there are suggestions in this book to help support these. Developing independence in personal hygiene is another key area and relevant health and safety issues are highlighted throughout the book. Some activities require more focused attention from children in order to develop concentration, and others require self-motivation and personal initiative. Care and concern for living things and for our environment are encouraged and children have opportunities to respond to their experiences through self-expression.

Language and Literacy

This important area of learning also pervades all the others. In order to be able to communicate effectively with others, children must be able not only to express themselves clearly with a growing vocabulary, but to listen attentively, too. Through their developing speaking and listening skills they are also able to respond to stories, rhymes, poems and songs.

In order to develop early book skills children should have access to a wide variety of quality fiction and non-fiction books and hence a comfortable, inviting, well-stocked reading area is a must. Children should have opportunities to handle and pretend-read books by themselves, look at them with friends, and share stories with supportive adults. See the resources section on page 60 for a list of books that support the activities in this book.

Additionally, through these and other experiences, children are becoming aware of the written word and its purpose in carrying information. Children should be given many opportunities to make home-made books using pictures, marks, symbols and letters, and to share them

with others. An area kept well supplied with a range of relevant equipment to stimulate mark-making and emergent writing should be another essential part of the nursery environment. While there are some specific activities involving book-making in this book, there are many others that you could extend to include personal or whole class picture-book-making to add to your reading area.

Mathematics

In order to promote confidence and enjoyment, it is essential that young children should experience early mathematics through the provision of a range of interesting play-based practical activities aimed at developing their concepts of shape, size, number, order, measurement and pattern, the main focus being on understanding. The use of mathematical language for counting, ordering, comparing and describing in order and communicating meaning is also crucial; children should hear adults using mathematical terms appropriate to the situation. This book includes activities that involve sorting, counting, sequencing, measuring, shopping and using both cardinal and ordinal numbers. The concept of measuring time is explored through meaningful investigations, such as the use of a sand timer for ensuring fair turns and timing when cooking, as opposed to the direct teaching of telling the time, which is not appropriate at this stage of development. A great deal of time-related vocabulary is also introduced and reinforced. Sequence and pattern are explored in ways relevant to the

young child's understanding, using observation to support learning. All learning is additionally reinforced by the introduction of play materials such as jigsaw puzzles and through investigation.

Science and Technology

This area of the curriculum focuses on children developing their awareness and understanding of the world around them, thus enabling them to make sense of their experiences. It incorporates the scientific and technological aspects of the early-years curriculum. Children are naturally curious about the world around them and need to be provided with opportunities to observe, investigate, experiment, question and hypothesise through carefully planned child-centred practical scientific investigations. The importance of careful, open-ended questioning by adults is crucial for developing children's thinking. Children should be presented with activities that encourage them to explore using all their senses, while being made aware of potential health and safety hazards and of the importance of food hygiene. Activities in this book include exploring change over time involving cooking, melting, freezing, and growing things.

Technological awareness is encouraged by designing, making and evaluating junk models or construction toys, using computers, and operating cassette recorders to listen to stories or taped interviews. In model-making, children should be encouraged to select their own materials and to handle implements safely. Evaluation of the suitability of a finished product for its intended purpose should also be encouraged, for example, if the

children have made a magnetic mouse to travel along a maze, they should test it to find out if it works and consider ways in which it might be improved.

Time and Place

This area of learning incorporates the historical and geographical aspects of the early years curriculum and focuses on children developing a growing awareness and understanding of their past and of the environment in which they live.

In this book children begin to develop a sense of time through activities intended to develop their awareness of their personal histories and past events. They are encouraged to reflect, reason and question through sharing celebrations, talking about family events, and using artefacts, photographs or pictures. Through recall activities or while interviewing visitors they are developing a growing vocabulary of time.

Through geographical investigations of their locality children develop their sense of place. They are developing their vocabulary of direction and location, becoming familiar with the names of natural and made features and of their uses. They are finding out about the effects of events in the natural world around them such as weather changes, and developing informed concern for their environment and for other living things. They find out about other people, their jobs, where they work and how they carry out their work in their daily routines. This book includes activities involving seasonal walks, weather investigations, and local explorations to help develop early geographical concepts.

Physical Development

This area of learning focuses on children's awareness of their bodies and how they function. Planned activities in Physical development are intended to develop co-ordination, strength, fitness and confidence. To enable gross motor development, activities should be provided to encourage physical skills such as running, jumping, hopping, rolling, stretching, curling, skipping, climbing, balancing, throwing, catching and kicking. Through these activities children can be made aware of the space around them and of others, in addition to the need to use both small and large equipment safely. Fine motor skills can be developed through the provision of activities that include holding and controlling a variety of implements, such as gluing, cutting, drawing, painting, threading, fitting and modelling.

Creative Development

Here, children are developing creativity through music, art and drama. They listen and respond to music and songs,

learning to handle instruments with care both through exploration and in conjunction with singing and shared music-making activities. The art area should be furnished with a wide range of materials including papers, paints, brushes, chalks and other resources. Children should be encouraged to explore and use a variety of media to express their ideas through art, investigating colour, shape, form and pattern in both two and three dimensions. Spontaneous use of drawing and painting is vital, but children should also have some opportunities to represent through making close observational drawings of artefacts, too.

Children can experience communication of ideas and feelings through interacting with others in imaginative role play situations using a range of props and resources, including dressing up clothes, small world toys and puppets. The home corner can be put to good use here, as it can be transformed to provide different environments according to your topic, such as the garden centre during the plant growth topic, or the castle in the story of 'Jack and the Beanstalk'. Imaginative role play is also invaluable in supporting children's personal and social development through encouraging turn-taking, sharing, co-operation, negotiation and awareness of how it feels to be someone else.

Planning activities

When planning any focused activity it is important to be aware of the intended learning. Having planned outcomes will make assessing what has been learned more specific. Note down in advance the intended learning; think about the resources you will use to support the learning process; consider carefully the language you will use to ensure the children understand what is required of them thus enabling them to respond accordingly. It goes without saying that it is essential to know your children well in order to be able to provide appropriate differentiation and challenge.

Planning focused learning

If trying something new, make an attempt at it yourself before you present it to the children in order to avoid any surprise pitfalls. Before beginning any focused activity, ensure that the other adults in the room are aware of what you will be doing and ask them to support the rest of the class so that you can concentrate on working with your group without too many distractions. The following list contains practical suggestions for preparing for an activity:

- Ensure that the working area is both safe and suitable for the purpose, for example covering a table top for a messy activity, or making sure that the cooker is in an appropriate position, and that you have enough space.
- Identify and collect together the resources you and the children will need. Ensure you have sufficient resources to complete the activity and, if appropriate, independent choice resources such as a selection of paper sizes and colours for the children to choose from.
- Know where any finished products will go. Have available a drying rack for wet paintings perhaps or a designated place for finished junk models.

- Ensure any implements needed are fit for their purpose, for example that the scissors will cut or that pencils are sharpened.
- Prepare ahead for possible accidents such as water spillages.
- Provide aprons to protect clothes if necessary; if these are colour-coded to specific activities such as blue aprons for water play, and red for painting, the children can find them for themselves.
- Have your notebook or assessment sheets and a pen to hand ready to record your observations.

Do, of course, encourage independence in the children in preparing for activities by asking questions such as 'What do you think we will need for..?' 'Which apron will you need?'

When the activity has been completed, encourage children to tidy up afterwards leaving the area ready for the next group of children to begin. They should be aware of where resources are kept and of the importance of checking that items are complete, for example, only returning finished jigsaw puzzles to their shelves. It helps if the children are aware of the purposes of different areas of the classroom – labels with picture symbols can help with this, such as a paintbrush and paint pot sign hanging over the designated painting area.

Assessing children's learning

Assessment of learning is essential as it informs future planning requirements and enables provision of different activities. It is therefore crucial that you are fully aware of your learning intentions in order to be able to assess the outcome for each individual child. Careful dated notes on each child's progress in the areas of learning provide evidence of attainment and it is also useful to retain samples of work such as pictures, emergent writing, and photographs to support your record keeping. Much assessment can be done through talking with children, particularly if you use open-ended questioning techniques.

Asking questions

Careful questioning is one way of being able to assess what a child knows or has learned. There is a particular skill in being able to pose questions in a way that enables the child to tell you what she/he thinks or believes. This useful technique involves the use of open-ended questions to which there is no one answer but a range of possible responses, and in which personal opinions are sought. These are particularly valuable in developing children's confidence as they remove the threat of giving the 'wrong' answer, which will often deter an uncertain child from responding in any depth. The activities throughout this book include suggested questions designed to encourage children to observe, predict, and hypothesise through stories and practical, play-based and child-centred activities.

The following show a variety of open-ended questions intended to help you to elicit more detailed responses:
- What can you see/hear/smell?
- How does it feel/taste?
- What else can you see now?
- What do you think will happen next?
- Why do you think that happened?
- Can you tell us about any changes?
- Why do you like that one best?
- Where do you think the water from that puddle has gone?
- What have you decided to do next?

Investigating the locality

Children learn a great deal through practical first-hand experiences, investigations and observations. A walk outdoors based around a planned theme such as a seasonal walk will support learning. It is a good idea to research the fieldwork yourself before you take the children out, to enable you to be aware of any safety hazards, such as roads, and to prepare fully your learning intentions. It goes without saying that any visit outside the nursery environment should be carefully planned to ensure the children's safety, and reference must be made to the nursery's policy on taking the children beyond the nursery grounds. Send a letter to carers and parents beforehand outlining the purpose of the activity and giving full details of the trip together with a consent form for them to sign and return giving their permission for you to take the children out. Appropriate supervision levels should be arranged to ensure the children's safety; they should be placed with an adult helper in very small groups.

Before you go out make sure others left at the nursery know who you are taking, where you are going, and roughly when you expect to arrive

back. Talk to adult helpers about the purposes of the activity and the kinds of question they might ask or be asked by the children. Ensure the children also understand the purpose of the trip, their expected behaviour and your reasons for it. Introduce them to their helpers and do not forget to give each helper a list of their group's names. It is a good idea to put a name badge on each child to help with identification. Do not forget to take a first aid pack and a list of useful telephone numbers with you in case of emergencies. As the trip progresses ensure that you and your assistants count the children as you move on from each area.

Visitors to the nursery

Inviting visitors in to talk with the children is a useful way of developing community involvement. It is also helpful to support children's learning in situations where visits are not possible. Visitors you could invite connected with the theme of Time might include:
- Older relations, such as grandparents, to talk about past events in their lives.
- Parents with their new baby.
- People from different cultures to talk about their food or celebrations.
- A clock maker or clock repairer
- The curator from a local museum
- People willing to talk about their jobs and routines, including people who work at night

If possible, talk to the visitors in advance about what you would like them to talk about and the kinds of question the children might ask. Suggest they bring in artefacts or pictures to focus the children's interest, and suggest they wear the clothes appropriate to their role. Prepare the children before the visitors arrive. Ensure they understand the difference between a statement, which is something we tell someone, and a question, in which someone gives an answer with information you want to know, and let them practise their questioning techniques by interviewing you first. Taping an interview with a visitor is a useful way of recording information for the children to access using a cassette recorder at a later date.

Try to invite a balanced representation of visitors to avoid reinforcing any stereotype.

Visitors should not be left alone with the children.

How to use this book

All About Time is divided into seven self-contained chapters each developing one avenue of the book's central theme. Each chapter has its own coloured band and its own contents list to help you identify which chapter you are in. The contents list gives you a summary of each activity to help you decide which activities to use. The materials needed for each activity are always found at the top.

Educational symbols
Each activity introduces one or more areas of learning. The symbols show you which areas are covered and the accompanying text gives you the specific aims.

 This symbol shows the activity will develop aspects of language and literacy

 This symbol shows the activity will develop aspects of science and technology

 This symbol shows the activity will develop aspects of creative development

 This symbol shows the activity will develop aspects of mathematics

 This symbol shows the activity will develop aspects of personal and social development

 This symbol shows the activity will develop aspects of physical development

 This symbol shows the activity will develop aspects of time and place

Each activity is numbered for easy reference.

The triangle and circle show you the suggested adult–child ratio for the activity.

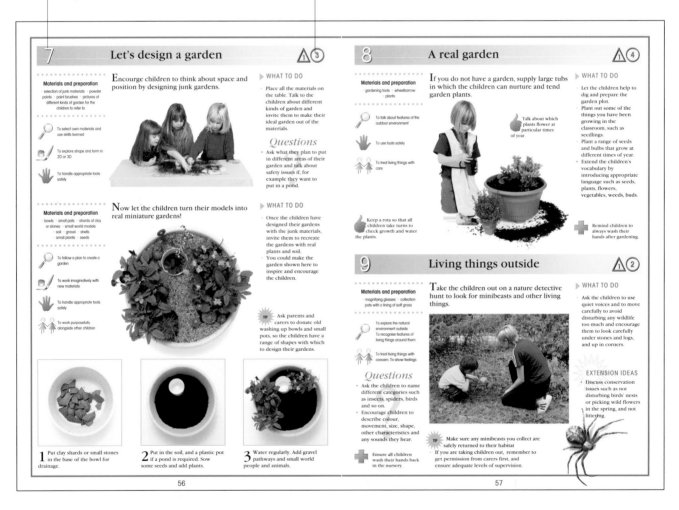

Additional symbols
Many activities have additional hints and tips or safety points. They are identified by the symbols shown below.

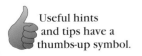 Useful hints and tips have a thumbs-up symbol.

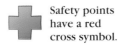 Safety points have a red cross symbol.

Breaking down the information
Each activity either has step-by-step instructions or bullet-pointed instructions under the heading 'What To Do'. Many activities also have suggested questions and extension ideas, also under the appropriate headings.

 TIP One or more helpful suggestions for increasing an activity's learning value have a star symbol.

Topic web

Each activity in this book is underpinned by one or more areas of learning. This topic web lists all the activities that develop each area of learning under the appropriate heading. Use this web when planning your curriculum to ensure the activities you use develop all areas of learning according to the particular early years guidelines you are following. This will help you create an educationally exciting and balanced theme that your children will love!

SCIENCE AND TECHNOLOGY

PERSONAL AND SOCIAL DEVELOPMENT

PHYSICAL DEVELOPMENT

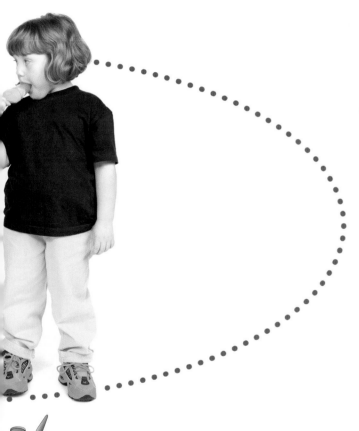

TIME AND ME

The activities in this chapter are designed to develop children's understanding of time in relation to themselves. This starts with an awareness of their birthdays and how old they are and then progresses to how they have changed since babyhood and how they continue to grow. There are incentives for children to reflect upon and share with others their experiences of both distant and recent past events in their own lives. The activities also provide opportunities for home-school liaison as some activities require resources from home such as photographs of the children when they were babies, and favourite toys from babyhood.

Activities in this chapter

1
What is a birthday?
Raising awareness of the meaning of birthdays through celebrating them in the nursery and singing a birthday song

2
How old am I?
Developing awareness of numbers in relation to themselves through making a collage birthday cake with the appropriate number of candles

3
My next birthday
Making collage elephants for the class birthday chart and using photographs of the children so that everyone can identify when their next birthdays will be

4
Growing taller
Using an ongoing height chart to measure and record children's growth over the year

5
Different clothes
An activity involving ordering by size using clothes from age 0–5

6
What can I remember?
Sharing past memories with others in a group circle and making a class photograph album to prompt children's recollections of events

7
What did I look like?
Looking at photographs of ourselves when we were babies and identifying how we have changed

8
How did I move?
Exploring stages in the development of movement from babyhood onwards

9
My favourite toy
Showing and talking about a favourite babyhood toy, and then drawing it from close observation

What is a birthday?

Raise awareness of the meaning of birthdays as you celebrate them at nursery.

Materials and preparation

photograph of birthday child · 3D model birthday cake with real candles · individual birthday cards

 To become aware of numbers

👍 Keep a list of children's birth dates on your notice board Remember to celebrate birthdays that come in the school holidays

Questions

- How old were you yesterday?
- How old are you now?
- How many years older are you?
- Do you think you have changed?
- How do you feel now it is your birthday?

▶ WHAT TO DO

- Explain that birthdays are special times when we celebrate how much time has passed in whole years since the day we were born.
- Invite the birthday child to talk about her birthday and how she is feeling. Clap her age now and then light the correct number of candles on the model cake.
- Sing 'Happy Birthday' then say 'Ready, Steady, BLOW!'
- Give her a card to take home from all her friends at nursery.

---

2 How old am I?

Children will enjoy making a collage cake and counting how many candles they need for it.

Materials and preparation

coloured paper · strips of coloured card · yellow tissue paper · scissors · glue

 To talk about their own experiences

 To handle scissors with increasing control

 To count using one to one correspondence

To use joining skills

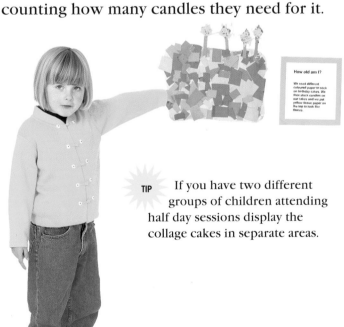

How old am I?

We used different coloured paper to stick on birthday cakes. We then stuck candles on our cakes and we put yellow tissue paper on the top to look like flames.

⭐ TIP If you have two different groups of children attending half day sessions display the collage cakes in separate areas.

▶ WHAT TO DO

- As each child has their birthday, invite them to make a collage birthday cake, cutting enough pretend candles from the card to stick on to it and adding flames made from torn tissue paper.
- Add it to the display of other collage cakes and involve the children in counting how many of them are the same age.

Questions

- How many candles do you need to stick on?
- How many children are four years old now?

Materials and preparation

12 elephants cut out of coloured paper
coloured tissue paper · glue
glue spreaders
photograph of each child

To listen to a story in a group

To use glue and spreaders with increasing control

To count in a practical activity
To name colours

To respond to own experiences of the world

This activity is based on the popular story 'Elmer' by David McKee, published by Red Fox.

TIP When making name labels for the months, colour code the seasons. You could write winter month labels in blue, spring in green, summer in red, and autumn in brown.

▶ WHAT TO DO

- Share the story of 'Elmer' and talk about special days and celebrations.
- Explain that they will be making an Elmer-style collage for each month of the year. Each Elmer will be labelled with a month and each child will attach a photograph of him/herself under the appropriate Elmer.
- Talk about all the patchwork colours that make up Elmer and encourage the children to choose the appropriate colours of tissue paper to stick on their Elmers.

TIP If possible, get groups of children with birthdays in the same month to work together on their particular birthday elephant to encourage co-operation
- If you have two groups, stick balloon shapes above each Elmer.
- Colour-code the balloon shapes into morning and afternoon groups and ask the children to stick their photographs into the appropriately coloured balloon shapes.

At the end of the session, stick all the Elmers in a row on the nursery wall. Label each Elmer with a month.

▶ WHAT TO DO

- At the beginning of the following session show the children the labelled Elmers.
- Ask the children to take it in turns to stick their photographs underneath the appropriate Elmer.
- Once all the children have stuck their photographs up, ask the questions below.

Questions

- Ask the children to name the months of the year and talk about the seasons
- How many children were born in the same month as you?
- In which month were most children born?

4 Growing taller

Make a height chart based on a plant or animal to make it really eye-catching.

Materials and preparation

height chart · name label for each child · Blu Tac · individual record cards

To take off/put on own shoes independently

To use some comparative mathematical language

To recognise own name

TIP Introduce comparative language such as tall/taller/tallest, taller than/shorter than as you measure the children

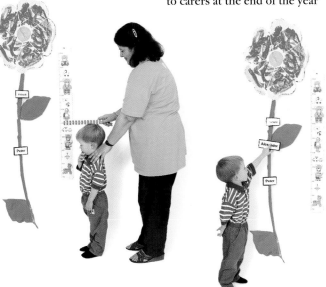

It's a good idea to keep individual records in case labels fall off, and to pass on to carers at the end of the year

WHAT TO DO

Ask the children to take off their shoes and then measure them against the chart, indicating their height by attaching the name labels with blu tac. Do this again two months later so that they can observe the changes.

EXTENSION IDEAS

When you take each child's final measurement at the end of the school year, measure their growth on a piece of paper and give them a variety of objects to compare the measurement against.

---

5 Different clothes

Use clothes as a visual aid to help children learn about how much they grow.

Materials and preparation

selection of clothes ranging in size from newborn to five years · washing line · clothes-pegs.
Peg five items of clothing on the line in order of size · laundry basket

To order by size

To name different types of clothes

EXTENSION IDEAS

- Use for sorting by other criteria, for example colour or type
- Share the book 'Mrs Mopple's Washing Line' by Anita Hewett, Red Fox.
- Convert the home corner into a launderette for imaginative role play

WHAT TO DO

Talk about the washing line and ask the children what they notice about the clothes and their sizes. Encourage them to sort clothes in the laundry basket by size and to put them in order.
· Introduce comparative language such as smaller than, next, biggest.

Inform carers of the purpose of the activity and ask them to help you to collect the clothes you need.

Questions

- Which is the smallest?
- Which is the largest?
- Which one do you think we should put on the washing line next?
- Could you wear this now?
- Who do you think wore this?

6   What can I remember?

Materials and preparation

teddy bear
photographs of the children taken on
special occasions

 To recall a past event in own life

 To take turns

 To talk about experiences and listen attentively

Questions

- Use time related language such as 'When I was a little girl a long time ago...' 'When you were a baby...' 'Last week...' 'Yesterday...' and so on.

Introduce this activity by talking about some of your childhood memories.

2 Make a class book with the photographs the children have brought in. Ask them to describe and write about their memories of the events photographed.

Ensure the children know that if they do not want to say anything, they can pass the teddy on to the next person.

1 Explain that you are going to pass a teddy round so that each child can take turns telling the group about a memory while holding the teddy.

TIP Give the children a little time for reflection before you begin to pass the teddy round, suggesting that they close their eyes while they are thinking about something they can remember

7   What did I look like?

Materials and preparation

children's baby photographs
photograph album   paper   pen

 To talk about past events in own lives

 To recognise own name

Write a note to parents asking them to bring in photographs of their children as babies for this activity.

Keep the photographs in an acetate film covered album so that they may be returned to carers undamaged

▶ **WHAT TO DO**

- Put the photographs in the album as the children bring them in, talking with them about how they have changed, and label each one with the child's name.
- Keep the album in the book corner and encourage the children to look at the pictures and to try to identify each other.

Questions

- How do you think you have changed?
- What can you do now that you couldn't do when you were a baby?
- Who do you think that is?

8 How did I move?

Materials and preparation

Arrange for carers and parents who have babies and toddlers to bring them into the nursery so that children can observe how they move

 To develop gross motor skills

 To respond imaginatively to what they hear

 To listen in a group

 To talk about past events in their own lives

EXTENSION IDEAS

Provide opportunities to further develop gross motor skills outdoors; for example, jumping, skipping, hopping, balancing, climbing.

This activity provides many opportunities to build on family links with the nursery.

How Many Days?

How many days has my baby to play?

Saturday, Sunday, Monday,

Tuesday, Wednesday, Thursday, Friday,

Saturday, Sunday, Monday.

Hop away, skip away,

My baby wants to play,

My baby wants to play every day!

👍 Encourage awareness of space and safety for themselves and others when moving around

▶ WHAT TO DO

- Teach the children the rhyme. Ask them to talk about how they think the baby in the rhyme plays.
- Introduce the children to the babies and toddlers and discuss with the children how they move.
- Encourage the children to explore movements as you prompt them with a given percussion signal, for example wriggling to a rattling sound.

TIP Use descriptive words for the movements and name body parts.
- Introduce descriptive language, such as wriggling, rolling, crawling, shuffling, toddling and walking, for the movements.

---

9 My favourite toy

Materials and preparation

toys children have brought in · paper · pencils

 To use a pencil with increasing control

 To make a representative drawing through observation

 To listen and respond to a story

 To talk about past events in their own life

This activity is based on the story 'Dogger' by Shirley Hughes, published by Red Fox.

👍 Do not forget to bring in one of your own and join in yourself!

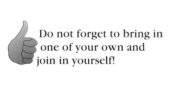

▶ WHAT TO DO

- Share the story 'Dogger' by Shirley Hughes, Bodley Head, and have a circle time where each child can show and talk about the toy they have brought.
- Make a display of the toys and invite the children to draw a picture of their toy.

Questions

Encourage the children to use their senses when describing their toys by asking questions such as
- What colour is it?
- How does it feel?
- Does it make any sounds?

TIME AND MY DAY

This chapter focuses on the patterns of children's usual daily routines and the reasons for them, including issues relating to personal hygiene and the need for rest and sleep. There is also an activity to show them that some days are special and therefore normal routines can alter to include a celebration. The activities also help to develop children's concepts of time in relation to the natural world and its effects upon our lives, with particular reference to night and day. There are opportunities to explore individual daily patterns and to share both fiction and non-fiction books.

Activities in this chapter

1
Morning activities
A sequencing card activity ordering four stages in a child's morning routine, incorporating the importance of both washing and dental hygiene

2
What do I do at bedtime?
A follow-up activity about bedtime routines involving sequencing events and making a zigzag book

3
What do I do at nursery?
This activity focuses on the nursery routine and involves children in looking at photographs of regular daily events and identifying them

4
Nursery celebrations
Creating an ongoing photograph album of special events that occur over the nursery year for children to remember and talk about

5
What day is it today?
Using a days of the week chart to identify today, yesterday and tomorrow

6
What did I do today?
An opportunity for children to recall the day's events and share them with others in a circle time

7
Daytime patterns
Using fiction and non-fiction books to find out more about daytime. This activity also focuses on the safety measures we need to be aware of when out in the sun

8
My shadow
This activity introduces the concept of sunlight and shadows through experiential play outside

9
What happens at night?
Finding out more about night-time, nocturnal creatures and people who work at night

10
Feeling safe at bedtime
An imaginative role-play activity that provides opportunities to explore bedtime routines and fears of the dark

Morning activities

Materials and preparation

one set of four picture sequencing cards, for example showing a child waking up in bed, getting dressed, washing, brushing his teeth

 To sing in a group

 To talk about own experiences

 To be aware of need for personal hygiene

 To sequence a pattern

Questions

- What do you think he does first/next?
- Why do we wash in the mornings?
- Why do we need to brush our teeth in the morning?

Use sequencing pictures to enable children to gain an awareness of their morning routines, and talk to them about how this may vary on weekends from weekdays.

Here We Go Round the Mulberry Bush

Here we go round the mulberry bush,

The mulberry bush, the mulberry bush

Here we go round the mulberry bush,

On a cold and frosty morning.

This is the way we wash our hands,

Wash our hands, wash our hands.

This is the way we wash our hands,

On a cold and frosty morning.

▶ WHAT TO DO

- Talk with the children about their own morning routines, then introduce the sequencing cards and talk about what is happening in the pictures. Let them sort the cards in order, accepting their own sequence if it is logical

 Let the children make their own morning routine cards.

What do I do at bedtime?

Materials and preparation

- one set of pictures depicting typical activities that form bedtime routines for each child • one home-made zigzag book for each child • pencils • crayons • glue

 To become aware that pictures carry meaning. To follow them from left to right

 To be aware of the need for personal hygiene

 To sequence a pattern

Use this activity to increase children's awareness of different bedtime routines.

▶ WHAT TO DO

- Ask the children to talk about their bedtime routines.
- Give each child a set of pictures and ask them to put them in order.
- Give each child a zigzag book. Ask them to stick the pictures in the correct order in their zigzag books.

EXTENSION IDEAS

- Adapt 'Here we go round the mulberry bush' to bedtime routines '...on a cold and frosty evening'.

Ensure the children know that it is perfectly acceptable to have different bedtime routines from their friends' routines.

What do I do at nursery?

Materials and preparation

Make a time line using photographs of key times in your nursery routine, for example: children arriving • playing • outdoor time • snack time • story time • going home • mount them on card and display them in sequence where children can see them easily

To function in a group beyond the family

To talk about own experiences

To recognise the pattern of the daily nursery routine

EXTENSION IDEA

- Provide additional sets of smaller photographs for the children to sort in order.

This activity will encourage children to think about everyday nursery activities.

1 Stage one could show taking coats off

2 Stage two could show the childern playing

3 Stage three could show snack time.

4 Stage four could show story time.

> WHAT TO DO

- Encourage children to refer to the time line to check the routine.
- Use time language such as 'At 11 o'clock we have our story time'.

Questions

- What are we doing now?
- What will happen next?
- What did we do when we first arrived?
- What happens last?
- What is your favourite time of the day?

Have the photographs enlarged to enable children to observe and discuss details

---

Nursery celebrations

Materials and preparation

Put together an album of photographs recording special events and celebrations at nursery over the year

To talk about own experiences

To talk about past events in own school life

To share with other children and adults.

Keep the album in the book corner for free access. Encourage the children to share it with each other.

You will need to collect photographs of special nursery occasions for this activity.

 Provide home-made books for children to record nursery memories in pictures and writing.

> WHAT TO DO

- Make the photograph album as described in the materials and preparation box.
- Share the album with groups or individuals and talk about their memories of the events and celebrations.

Questions

- Do you remember when ..?
- What was happening when..?
- Who came ..?
- Why/when did we do this?'

What day is it today?

Use activities held on specific days to help children to understand the days of the week.

Materials and preparation
Make 'days of the week' chart and 'today' label with Blu Tac on back
• laminate photographs of typical nursery activities

 To name days of the week

 To count to seven

Laminate the chart to make it more durable.

Use a different colour for each weekday, but make Saturday and Sunday both black to highlight the weekend days.

EXTENSION IDEAS
• Make stick on cards and identify 'yesterday' and 'tomorrow'.
• Share the book 'Jasper's Beanstalk' by Butterworth and Inkpen.
• Recite the rhyme 'Monday's child is fair of face'.

WHAT TO DO
• Count and name all the days of the week using the chart, identifying which days we come to nursery and the two weekend days.
• Every day, during group times, identify the day and move the arrow so that it points to the correct word.
• Introduce the activity photographs to the children and talk to them about when each activity takes place.
• At the end of each session, invite the children to stick the relevant photographs on to the chart to show what they have done at nursery that day.

What did I do today?

This activity can be used as a follow-on to What can I remember (6) page 16.

Materials and preparation
• teddy bear • objects children have played with and made during session

 To listen attentively and talk about own experiences

 To wait for own turn to speak

You could start off the activity by talking about something all the children have taken part in, such as creating collage Elmer elephants.

WHAT TO DO
• Explain that we are going to have a 'Pass the teddy' circle time. Whoever is holding teddy will have a turn to tell us about something that they have done today and everyone else will listen. Give them a short time to think about what they want to say and begin the session by saying something yourself.
• Let the children use the objects as prompts.

If someone does not want to say anything they just pass teddy on to the next child

Daytime pictures

* selection of fiction and non-fiction books about daytime – see the resources section on page 60 * paper * brightly coloured paints * paint brushes

 To recognise features of the natural world

 To be aware of safe practices when out in the sun

Questions

Extend vocabulary to include words such as morning, day, afternoon, shine, rays, sunlight, and ask:
* What can we do to protect our skin from sunburn?
* What can we do to protect our eyes?

This discussion activity will encourage the children to paint all kinds of bright picture.

▶ WHAT TO DO

* Talk about things we can do during the day.
* Discuss what makes daylight and find pictures of the sun in the books.
* Explain that, even if we cannot see it, the sun is always there.
* Talk about the dangers of bright sunshine and what we can do to protect our eyes and skin from it.
* Ask the children to paint what they like to do on sunny days. Make a display of their paintings and scribe their comments as a record of the acitivity.

👍 Learn the song 'The sun has got his hat on' and paint suns with hats on or sunny day pictures

---

My shadow

 To investigate sunlight and shadows

 To be willing to explore new learning

To run, jump, hop, skip

Questions

* Can you make your shadow run/skip/jump?
* Can you get away from your shadow?
* Can you make it go behind you?
* Can you make your shadow's hand touch your friend's shadow's hand?
* What other shadows can you see?

You could introduce this activity by watching the beginning of the film 'Peter Pan' and talking about Peter's shadow.

✚ Seek permission from carers if you plan to take children out beyond the nursery and ensure adequate levels of supervision.

👍 Take the children out on a cloudy day and ask why they think there are no shadows

▶ WHAT TO DO

* Take the children out on a sunny day to look at the shadows around them and to explore their own shadows.
* Encourage them to experiment to see what their shadows can do.
* After discussion, explain that we can see the shadows because something is blocking out the sun's light.
* Take the children out at different times of the day to observe how their shadows change.

What happens at night?

Use this activity to make children aware that, while they sleep at night, others are active.

Collect books to share such as: 'Can't you sleep little bear?' • 'The baby who wouldn't go to bed' • 'In the middle of the night' • 'Peace at last' See the resources section for more details

 To recognise the daily pattern

 To enjoy books

 To sing the rhyme on their own

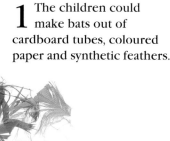

1 The children could make bats out of cardboard tubes, coloured paper and synthetic feathers.

2 Owls could be modelled out of clay. Once the clay has dried out, the children can paint them.

EXTENSION IDEA

Invite someone who works at night to come in to talk about their daily and night-time routine.

▶ **WHAT TO DO**

- Share the stories and talk about their content.
- Share your own experiences of night-time and talk about people who work at night.
- Introduce vocabulary such as evening, twilight, dark, midnight, stars, moonlight, planets, nocturnal, diurnal.
- Explain what nocturnal creatures are and ask the children to think of some they know.
- Let the children make models of nocturnal creatures.

10

Feeling safe at bedtime

This role-play activity heightens children's awareness of bedtime routines.

Materials and preparation

Convert home corner into bathroom/bedroom area for role play. Supply resources such as: nightwear • slippers • dressing gowns • flannel • towel • toothbrushes • story books – for example, 'Tell me Something Happy Before I Go To Sleep' by Joyce Dunbar and Debi Glion, Doubleday • soft toys • empty hot-water bottles • bedding • torches

 To use imagination in role play

 To recognise features of the world at night

 To express feelings

Extend vocabulary and role play by joining in yourself.

Twinkle, Twinkle

Twinkle, twinkle, little star,

How I wonder what you are;

Up above the world so high,

Like a diamond in the sky;

Twinkle, twinkle, little star,

How I wonder what you are.

▶ **WHAT TO DO**

- Talk about different bedtime routines and the people involved.
- Agree with the children the roles they could take and discuss a specific bedtime routine they can act out.
- Encourage them to tell bedtime stories or sing 'Twinkle, Twinkle, Little Star' to each other.

Questions

- What would mummy/daddy/nanny/you do next?
- Why do we brush our teeth before bedtime?
- Please can you tell me a story?

TIME AND FAMILIES

This chapter contains a range of activities designed to help children to develop their understanding of past events in relation to themselves and their families, and the variety of celebrations and their purposes. There are opportunities for family involvement and for questioning to find out information, as well as for raising awareness of other cultures. Practical and sensory investigations through practical comparisons of old and new artefacts and pictures are included to stimulate historical enquiry. It is important to ensure that you are aware of each child's own particular home circumstances and to convey positive attitudes towards them, adapting activities where necessary.

Activities in this chapter

1   People in my family

This activity will encourage children to think about family relationships.

Materials and preparation

home-made books, pencils, crayons, and a variety of doll's house dolls, for example a baby, child, parent, grandparent

 To follow the left-right directional sequence in making their book

 To talk about their families

EXTENSION IDEAS

- Ask the children to bring in photographs of their family members to add to their books.

 Ensure you are aware of children's family circumstances and adapt the activity accordingly.

WHAT TO DO

- Look at the doll's house dolls discussing their possible relationships and putting them in order of age.
- Encourage the children to talk about people in their own families. Then ask them to draw pictures of some family members in the books, starting with the youngest. In this way, they can make their own, individual family books.

Questions

- Who do you think is the youngest/oldest?
- Who is the youngest/oldest in your family?

---

2   Animal life cycles

This activity helps children think about the passage of time through life cycles.

Materials and preparation

variety of animal life cycle jigsaw puzzles

 To become aware of change through a life cycle

 To fit puzzles pieces together with control

To match puzzle pieces

1 Stage one, a hen lays an egg.

2 Stage two, the chick hatches from the egg.

3 Stage three, the chick grows into a hen.

4 Stage four, the hen is old enough to lay eggs.

Questions

Extend vocabulary according to the subject by using the correct terminology, and ask questions such as:
- What comes first?
- What happens next?

WHAT TO DO

- Lay out the jigsaws.
- Look at each jigsaw in turn. Play with it, talking about the changes that occur over time.

TIP Try to bring a variety of life cycle jigsaws covering a range of levels of difficulty, such as baby to adult, frog spawn to frog, egg to bird, caterpillar to butterfly.

When they were children

 To listen attentively

 To ask questions to find out information

 To talk in turn and work purposefully alongside other children

Invite children's grandparents and other elderly family members into the nursery to talk about their childhood.

👍 Ensure the children understand what a question is before the visit; explain someone has to give an answer to a question.

👍 Tape record the conversation to enable the children to listen to it again at a later date.

EXTENSION IDEAS

- Teach children old playground games to play at outdoor time.
- Make thank you pictures to send to the visitor.

▶ WHAT TO DO

- Invite grandparents and other elderly relatives into the nursery to talk about their childhood. Ask them to bring in photographs and any old toys they may have.
- Prepare questions to ask with the children before the visitor arrives.
- Introduce the visitor and let her/him show and talk about anything she/he has brought along
- Let the children ask questions in turn. Encourage them to think about how things have changed. Ensure that the children have an equal amount of time to ask questions.

Make a class museum

Materials and preparation

Collection of artefacts such as: old toys · books · photographs
· Provide additional resources such as: labels · pencils · paper · dusters · cash register · tickets

 To observe through imaginative play

 To recognise features of objects in the made world

 To treat resources with care and concern

TIPS Encourage children to design and make tickets, labels and lists for the museum
- Inform carers of the purpose of this activity and invite them to loan non-precious items for display in the class museum.

Convert your home corner into a museum for this activity.

➕ Remember to remove any sharp objects from your display, such as a sewing machine needle.

EXTENSION IDEA

- Take the children out on a brief focused visit to a local museum to look at old toys.

▶ WHAT TO DO

- Identify roles with the children – ticket seller, curator, visitors – and discuss what they do.
- Support the children in taking fair turns in these roles, extending imaginative play by joining in yourself.
- Encourage careful handling of the artefacts by the curator.

Questions

Use correct terminology, such as curator, display, exhibition, and explain their meanings. Ask questions like:
- How much does it cost to get in?
- What was this used for?
- Who do you think used it?

Valuing old possessions

 To listen in a group

 To express own feelings

You could ask the children to bring in their most valued old possession for this activity.

Questions

· How do you think she felt when..?
· Do you have something old you would like to tell us about?
· How would you feel if..?

This acitivity is based on 'The Patchwork Cat' by Nicola Bayley, published by Red Fox.

▶ **WHAT TO DO**

· Share the story, focusing on how the cat felt when she thought her patchwork was lost, even though it was old and dirty. Ask the children if they have a special old thing they would be sad to lose, allowing some time for reflection
· Invite each child to talk about a precious possession and how they feel about it. Accept all the children's responses and thank them for sharing it with the group.

Introduce vocabulary such as special, precious.

Comparing old and new

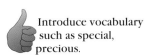

 To use a growing vocabulary to express own thoughts

 To look closely at similarities and differences

Set up a display of old and new toys for this activity in which children learn to compare.

TIP Include new vocabulary such as fluffy, soft, squashy, rough, hard, solid, fur, paws, worn, curve, round, and straight, as you discuss and draw the bears.

EXTENSION IDEAS

· Involve the children's families by asking them to bring in old and new toys, labelled with their names and those of their owners. If a toy has an interesting history invite its owner to come in and tell the children about it.

▶ **WHAT TO DO**

· Ask the children to examine and describe the new teddy. Repeat with the older one.
· Let them choose a teddy to draw, encouraging close observation for details as they work.
· Introduce the old and new display and talk about all the different kinds of toy.

Share the story 'Old Bear' by Jane Hissey. Red Fox Books, with the children.

7   Families in the past

Materials and preparation
- a print of an old painting of a family, or an old family photograph

To listen in a group

To talk about their own observations

To observe through art

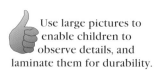

Use large pictures to enable children to observe details, and laminate them for durability.

This activity encourages children to compare their families with families in the past.

Questions
- What are they wearing?
- Who do you think they were?
- What are they doing?
- Do you/does mummy wear clothes like that now?
- Include vocabulary such as then, now, a long time ago, nowadays, recently, old-fashioned, modern, different, comfortable, uncomfortable

▶ WHAT TO DO

- Look closely at the picture and encourage the children to tell you what they can see and to ask questions. Encourage comparisons between what they see in the picture and how things are different now.

---

8   How they used to live

Materials and preparation
Variety of past everyday artefacts such as:
flat iron · clothes · books · sepia and black and white photographs · sewing machine · pieces of card to use as labels · marker pen

To explore objects and talk about when they were used

To explore new learning

To use a growing vocabulary to express thoughts

Questions
- What is it made of?
- What do you think it was used for?
- When do you think it was used?
- Who do you think would have used it?
- What do you think it is?
- Do we use it nowadays?

You could involve the children's families in this activity by asking them to bring in old, everyday objects.

EXTENSION IDEA
- Encourage the children to draw or paint the objects from close observation.

▶ WHAT TO DO

- Put the objects on a table and encourage the children to investigate them, describe them, and ask questions.
- As the children explore each object, record their comments. Label each object on a piece of card and scribe the chidren's comments.

Remember to remove any sharp objects from your display, such as a sewing machine needle.

Family trees

Materials and preparation

magazine pictures of families – be aware of the children's different ethnic origins · scissors · glue · paper · coloured pencils · marker pen

 To use scissors with increasing control

 To use comparative mathematical language

TIP Use comparative mathematical language such as taller/shorter, bigger/smaller, older/younger.
· Name possible relationships between people in the magazines and pictures.

This activity prompts children to understand the idea of different generations, and to talk about all kinds of family unit and ethnic origin.

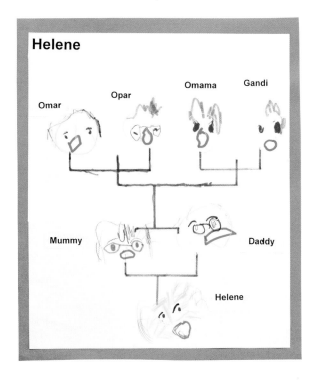

Helene

Omar · Opar · Omama · Gandi

Mummy · Daddy

Helene

▶ WHAT TO DO

· Talk with the children about people in their own families, then look at the pictures and make family collage pictures.
· Make a family tree with the children based on the characters in a storybook they are familiar with.
· Let the children make their own family trees, ensuring that you are sensitive to their family circumstances.

Family position

Materials and preparation

'You'll Soon Grow Into Them Titch' by Pat Hutchins, Red Fox · selection of toy baby and adult animals

 To listen attentively and respond to a story

 To express own feelings

 To use comparative mathematical language

TIP Allow some time for reflection first.
· Use comparative vocabulary such as younger/older taller/shorter bigger/smaller.

This activiy is based on the story book 'You'll Soon Grow Into Them Titch' by Pat Hutchins.

▶ WHAT TO DO

· Share the story, asking the children how they think Titch might be feeling as you show the pictures.
· Introduce the animals and ask the children to comment on how the baby animals may feel.
· Follow this up by having a 'pass the teddy' circle time (see page 16 activity 7) to share thoughts about what it feels like to be small in our world

Questions

· How do you think he is feeling?
· How can you tell?
· Would you like to wear old clothes all the time?

11 Planning a celebration

Materials and preparation

· range of information and picture books showing people taking part in celebrations · pencils · crayons

 To respond to cultural events

 To use pictures, symbols, letters to convey meaning

 To talk about past and present events in own lives and record them

 If children are going to taste food, inform parents and carers of ingredients beforehand in case of any allergies.

The activities on these pages show you how to prepare a Thanksgiving Celebration. Adapt them to suit any celebration appropriate to the time of year you wish to focus on.

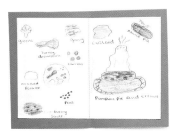 

▶ WHAT TO DO

· Look at pictures and resources connected with the celebration you are investigating and identify the kinds of food associated with it.
· Ask the children to draw their ideas for the menu; some children could also try to label their pictures

Carers may be willing to come in to help you prepare food for particular festivals.

Make sure that you are aware of any religious restrictions on the food that some children can eat.

12 Preparing a celebration

Materials and preparation

For the filling: a small pumpkin · two eggs · 175 ml double cream · 60 g caster sugar · tsp ginger · 30 ml black treacle · ready-made shortcrust pastry · saucepan · potato masher · rolling pin · pastry board · pastry cutter · spoons · four individual pastry tins

 To talk about change

 To respond to cultural events

Choose one element from the menu to prepare with the children.

▶ WHAT TO DO

· To make pumpkin pies, follow steps one to four below. Bake the pumpkin pies for 40 minutes at 180°C (350°F, Gas 4).

 Ensure children are aware of safe practices when the cooker is on, and of the dangers of burns and scalds when cooking.

 Inform carers of the ingredients beforehand in case of any allergies.

1 Dice the pumpkin and boil for 20 minutes. Add the other ingredients. Let the children mash everything.

2 Show the children how to roll out the pastry. Let them join in, allowing each child to use the rolling pin.

3 Allow them to cut out individual pastry cases and then put them in the greased bun tins.

4 Let them spoon the filling into the cases. An adult should put the pies in the oven to bake.

Materials and preparation

· range of books, pictures, puzzles and other resources relevant to the festival being celebrated ·

 To talk about events in own life.
To explore and select own materials

 To show ability to initiate new ideas

 To develop an awareness of other cultures

TIPS Be aware of the range of festivals celebrated by your nursery families over the year and keep a calendar of key events/dates.
· Remember that some festival dates are fixed, others are movable.

EXTENSION IDEAS

· Invite children's relatives to come in and talk about particular festivals and how they celebrate them.
· Let the children design and make greetings cards and 3D models, such as Divali candles, relevant to the festivals.
· Use samples of the children's work to add to, and enhance the informative display.

Inform carers of the ingredients beforehand in case of any allergies.

Now the children have planned and prepared for their celebration make sure you have a big party to celebrate!

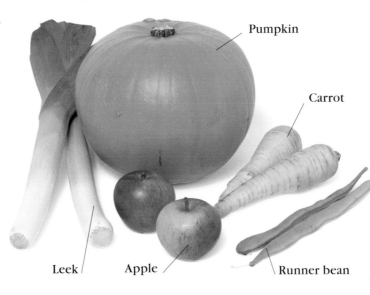

Pumpkin

Carrot

Leek

Apple

Runner bean

Ensure that all the children in the nursery join in the celebration. Don't forget to give them their pumpkin pies to eat!

▶ WHAT TO DO

· Shortly before the celebration, set up a display of relevant pictures, books, cards and artefacts and encourage the children to look at it and ask questions about the artefacts. If you are celebrating the American custom of Thanksgiving in November, be sure to include seasonal vegetables to show the purpose of the festival – to celebrate the harvest and also to offer thanks for everything that we have.
· Around the date of the celebration talk about it with the whole group.

TIP Explain the purpose of the activity to carers who will be celebrating around the time of each event and invite them to contribute artefacts or information.

MEASURING TIME

The activities in this chapter focus children's attention on how we measure time objectively in our world. There are opportunities to investigate a range of different timepieces, think about the mechanisms that drive them, and to talk about their particular purposes. The concept of why we need to be able to measure time objectively is also explored through a range of practical activities. Children are encouraged to gain their own sense of time by, for example, thinking about what they do in relation to the time of day, finding out how much they can accomplish within one minute and noticing seasonal changes.

Activities in this chapter

1
How do we measure time?
Looking at a variety of different timepieces and identifying situations in which they could be used

2
Looking closely at a clock
By choosing a timepiece to draw from close observation, children will extend their knowledge as to how it works

3
Hickory, Dickory, Dock
Introduce the concept of magnetism using this popular rhyme as a starting point

4
Make a magnetic mouse
Involving children in designing and making a grandfather clock, and a mouse to travel up and down it using magnetism

5
Cogs and wheels
Observe the workings of an old mechanical clock and use a cogs and wheels construction set to investigate the mechanism

6
A class clock repair shop
An imaginative role-play activity in which children are encouraged to discuss the workings of different timepieces

7
In the daytime
Using time-related vocabulary to help children to identify daily patterns and sequence of activities

8
When will it be my turn?
Introducing the concept of accurate timing using a sand timer to ensure fair turns

9
At the stroke of midnight
An imaginative activity to help develop gross motor skills and expressive ability

10
In one minute
A practical activity to investigate how much children can do in one minute, to give them a sense of time

1   How do we measure time?

Materials and preparation

Collect a variety of manufactured objects by which we objectively measure time, for example: wrist watch
- stop watch • alarm clock
- digital clock • mantel clock
- sand timer • diary

 To talk about own experiences

 To recognise features of made objects

 To use mathematical language

Questions

- When would we want to use this one?
- How do you think this one works?

Ask carers to bring in a selection of time pieces for this activity.

▶ **WHAT TO DO**

- Observe, investigate, name and talk about the clocks, noticing both the similarities and differences.

👍 Supply appropriate vocabulary such as dial, hands, long, short, face, hours, minutes, seconds, numbers, digital.

EXTENSION IDEA

- Collect natural materials appropriate to the season and introduce the concept of measuring the year by the four seasons.

---

2   Looking closely at a clock

Materials and preparation

- selection of timepieces as suggested in activity above • paper • pencils

 To use a growing vocabulary

 To recognise numbers to 12

 To observe through art

 To recognise features of made objects

 To use a pencil with increasing control

This activity can be used as a follow on to How do we measure time? (1) page 33

▶ **WHAT TO DO**

- Invite the children to choose a clock to draw, then encourage them to look closely, checking for details as they draw.
- Reinforce vocabulary already introduced and encourage additional mathematical language, such as round, square, top bottom, curved, straight.

Questions

- What is that number?
- Can you see the number 4/5/6? and so on.

EXTENSION IDEAS

- Extend the activity by making a clock with hands that can be moved.

3 Hickory Dickory Dock

Materials and preparation

Home-made cardboard clock and mouse – see (4) below for instructions on how to make these

 To move the magnet with control

 To use vocabulary to express thoughts

 To ask questions to find out how things work

 To recognise the number 1

Questions

- Can you make the mouse run up/down the clock?
- How did you do it?
- Can you make it go round the dial?
- Why do you think it is happening?

This activity will seem like magic until you explain the magnet you are holding behind the clock is drawing the paper clipped mouse upwards.

▶ WHAT TO DO

- Teach the children 'Hickory Dickory Dock'. Sing the rhyme together.
- Show the children the clock and mouse, and let them experiment with the resources to discover how they can make the mouse move up and down the clock.
- Use appropriate vocabulary such as magnetic, attract, stick.

EXTENSION IDEAS

- Draw mazes showing the pathway from a mouse hole to a piece of cheese on thin card and encourage the children to make their mice travel along from left to right to reach the cheese.

---

4 Make a magnetic mouse

Materials and preparation

- tracing paper • thin card • thick card
- marker pen • scissors • split pins
- magnet • paper clip • sticky backed plastic • sticky tape

 To explore form in 2D

 To explore and select materials.
To use scissors with increasing control

Use the templates on page 62 to help you make this magnetic mouse and grandfather clock with the children.

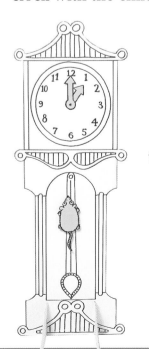

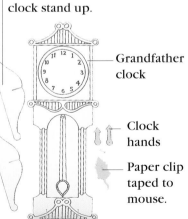

Feet to make clock stand up.

Grandfather clock

Clock hands

Paper clip taped to mouse.

1 Attach the clock hands to the centre of the clock face using a split pin.

▶ WHAT TO DO

- Enlarge and trace the relevant templates on page 62 on to the pieces of card.
- Cut out all the elements of the clock, and ask the children what they think each element is for.
- Follow steps one to three to assemble the clock and mouse.

2 Slide the thick card feet up the two slits cut in the base of the clock to make it stand up properly.

3 Cover all the elements with sticky-backed plastic to make them durable.

5   Cogs and wheels

Materials and preparation

- cogs and wheels construction set from a pre-school supplier • old mechanical clock with the workings exposed

 To talk about observations and ask questions to find out how things work
To use technology to support learning

 To handle construction equipment with increasing control

Investigate mechanisms using a cog and wheels set to promote interest in construction.

Bring in any extra pictures or information you have on clock mechanisms.

▶ WHAT TO DO

- Let the children experiment with the construction set, noticing which way the wheels are turning.
- Encourage the children to investigate and observe the workings of the old clock.
- Supply vocabulary such as cogs, wheels, turn, rotate.

Questions

- Which way is this wheel turning?
- Is the wheel touching it going the same way?

---

6   A class clock repair shop

Materials and preparation

- cogs and wheels set • old and new timepieces • clocks the children have made out of junk • cash register • paper • pencils
Include appropriate junk materials to create a workshop area, such as:
  - card • paper plates • pencils
  - felt-tipped pens • split pins
  - scissors • glue

 To learn about numbers through practical experiences

 To handle tools and materials safely and with increasing control

 To be willing to explore new learning

TIP   Invite a clock maker in to talk about what their job involves.
- Provide paper plates and sticky paper numerals for clock faces and pre-cut long and short hands for ease of usage

Convert your home corner into a clock repair shop for this activity.

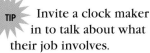

▶ WHAT TO DO

- Identify roles such as clock repairer, sales assistant, clock maker and customer, and encourage imaginative role play. Suggest that clock makers might like to design and make clocks with moving hands in the workshop.

Questions

- What is wrong with it?
- How much will it cost to repair?
- What type of clock are you going to make?
- Do you have any alarm clocks for sale please?
- Can you find a way to make the hands move?

7   In the daytime

Materials and preparation

- pictures or photographs of children doing everyday activities at various times of the day

 To sequence daily events

 To talk about events in own lives

Questions

- Why can't we do this at night time?
- Why don't we have a long sleep during the daytime?
- What is your favourite time of the day?

You could also try this activity on a Monday morning so that the children can talk about their weekend daytime activities.

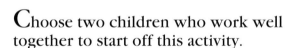
Setting off on a trip could signify the start of daytime activities.

▶ WHAT TO DO

- Encourage the children to talk about their own daytime activities, then look at the pictures and talk about the order they could be put into.

TIP   Use time-related vocabulary such as morning, midday, afternoon, evening, sunrise, sunset.

EXTENSION IDEAS

- Ask children to draw or paint their favourite daytime activities.

---

8   When will it be my turn?

Materials and preparation

- set a program up on the computer
- five minute sand timer

To take fair turns and share with another child

a b   To recognise own name

To use technology to support learning

To develop a concept of measuring time

Questions

- Ask them to suggest other ways of taking fair turns and why it is important to do so.

Choose two children who work well together to start off this activity.

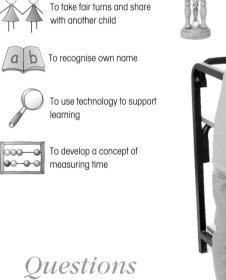

▶ WHAT TO DO

- Invite two children to the computer. Talk about how they could use it, taking fair turns.
- Show them the timer and explain how to use it.
- Ask one child to talk about what is happening as the sand trickles through the timer.
- Explain that, while one child plays on the computer, the other child can mark the time passing by observing the sand passing through the timer.
- Tell them that they can use the timer to measure fair turns at the computer. For longer periods of time, the sand timer can be turned. The children count the turns to make sure that they spend the same amount of time at the computer.

9 — At the stroke of midnight

Materials and preparation

toy puppets • large clock face • a clear space • drum • Jack in the box • rag doll • soldier • soft toy • drum

To count within 12

To move showing an awareness of space

To use imagination through dance

Questions

- What does this sound make you feel like doing?
- How do you think the soldier would move?

This imaginative activity can be used to help develop children's gross motor skills, and to encourage them to practise counting.

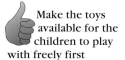
Make the toys available for the children to play with freely first

EXTENSION IDEA

Leave the toys and instruments available to encourage children to explore imaginative dance either individually or in small groups.

▶ WHAT TO DO

- Give the children the animal puppets and ask them to role play the animals coming to life.
- Introduce the toys. Talk about their features and how they move.
- Ask the children to curl up on the floor as if they were asleep.
- Make up a simple narrative about the toys coming to life at the stroke of midnight.
- Show the clock face set to midnight and ask the children to help you to count the twelve strokes.
- At the stroke of twelve, bang the drum and ask the children to move in the manner of their chosen toys.

---

10 — In one minute

Materials and preparation

one minute sand timer • resources for the activities such as: spade • sand • bucket • ball

To count orally

To use a range of equipment with increasing physical skill

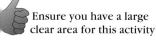
Ensure you have a large clear area for this activity

TIP Let the children explore the 'feel' of a minute first by waiting for the sand to trickle through the timer, or by watching the second hand travel around a clock dial.

Children will enjoy this physical activity that gives them a sense of how long a minute lasts.

Spend some time warming the children up before this activity

▶ WHAT TO DO

- Ask one child to estimate first, for example, 'How many spadefuls of sand do you think you would be able to put in a bucket in one minute?
- Set the timer, then count together as she puts sand in her bucket, and compare the results.
- Repeat with a different activity, such as throwing and catching a ball.

Questions

- Did a minute feel like a long time?
- What other activities do you think you can do in one minute?

TIME AND MY YEAR

This chapter focuses children's attention on the yearly cycle. They learn the names of the months of the year in our calendar through using their class birthday chart, and links with seasonal changes are made through outdoor observations and investigations. They are also encouraged to use natural materials to help them to identify the time of the year, and to notice weather and temperature changes in different seasons. Sequencing activities are used to reinforce understanding, in addition to practical experiences involving simple forms of recording and role-play situations.

Activities in this chapter

1
What month is it?
Using the class birthday chart to count and name the months of the year, and to identify the current month

2
What is happening outside?
Going out for a walk in the nursery grounds or in a local park to observe seasonal change in the natural environment

3
The four seasons
A sequencing activity in which children investigate the yearly pattern of the four seasons

4
Changing seasons
Reinforce knowledge of the four seasons using sequencing puzzles, then make a display to change with the seasons

5
What is the weather like?
Using a weather and 'days of the week' chart to promote discussion about current weather conditions and extend descriptive vocabulary

6
Make a weather chart
Making a class weather chart to record weather changes over the period of a week

7
Tomorrow's weather
Making a weather map with pictorial symbols to encourage children to predict the weather for tomorrow to others

8
Make a weather map
An opportunity for children to make their own maps and symbols for recording and forecasting the weather

9
Our weather centre
Set up an outdoor weather centre to record the weather conditions and convert the home corner into an indoor class weather centre

10
What shall I wear today?
A practical activity involving children in the class weather centre dressing up appropriately for the weather conditions forecast

What month is it?

To name months of the year and know that they are a time sequence

To count to 12

U se the Elmer birthday elephants made in My next birthday (3) page 14 for this activity.

September

In the autumn, you could collect evergreen and deciduous leaves.

Pine cone

Acorns

Deciduous leaves

WHAT TO DO

- Count and name the months of the year using the birthday elephants. Ask the children to name the current month.
- Explain which season the current month is in, then show the natural seasonal materials that you have collected.
- Discuss which materials are abundant in that season, such as daffodils in spring, roses in summer, conkers in autumn and holly in winter.

Questions

- Which month is it now?
- What is next month?
- What was last month?
- How many months are there in one year?

EXTENSION IDEA

Help children to identify which season they were born in by colour coding the month labels by the different seasons.

What is happening outside?

To talk about own experiences

To explore seasonal change in the natural environment

Inform carers about the outdoor excursion beforehand so that you have their permission and the children are dressed appropriately on the day.

T his activity can be run as a follow on to What month is it? (1) page 39.

WHAT TO DO

- Go for a walk outdoors to observe what is happening to trees and other natural objects.
- Talk about changes in weather and discuss when it is most likely to rain, snow and so on.

Plan to do this every season to identify and explore the changes.

EXTENSION IDEA

Give the children strips of coloured paper to match to natural materials, such as colours to match to fallen leaves in the autumn.

Questions

- What can you see?
- What colours are the leaves?
- What is happening?
- Which season is it?
- What is the weather like?
- How do you feel?
- Can you hear anything?

The four seasons

Materials and preparation

Make one set of four sequencing cards showing a tree in the spring, summer, autumn and winter

  Can use a growing vocabulary to express thoughts

  To respond to experiences of the world

  To recognise changes in the natural world

Introduce this activity by taking the children on a walk to look at trees near the nursery.

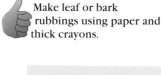

- What is happening to the tree in this picture?
- Which season do you think it might be?
- Which will come next?

 Make leaf or bark rubbings using paper and thick crayons.

TIP You could also use a seasonal jigsaw puzzle for this activity
- If you have, for example, a horse chestnut tree in your grounds make your sequencing cards link to that kind of tree.

WHAT TO DO

- Ask the children to look at the pictures and put them in order.
- Develop vocabulary to include buds, blossom, fruit, bare and so on.

Tell carers about the excursion beforehand. Ensure that the adult-to-child ratio allows for adequate supervision.

Changing seasons

Materials and preparation

- brown paper or corrugated card for tree trunk · stapler · tissue paper · assorted paper · felt-tipped pens · crayons

  To talk about experiences

  To recognise patterns and change in the natural world

  To explore colour, shape and form in 2D

Introduce this activity by showing the children a seasonal sequencing puzzle to help them identify changes.

Add weather symbols around the tree that are typical for that season, such as sunshine in summer.

Questions

- Are the leaves still green on the trees outside?
- Have you noticed any other changes?

WHAT TO DO

- On a display board, create a large tree trunk Leave room around it to add branches, leaves, blossom and so on.
- Identify the current season with the children and ask what they think needs to go on the tree.
- Decorate the tree as appropriate for the season – for example, with leaf rubbings, leaf prints, tissue blossom or apple prints. Try to create a tree that you have in your grounds or that most children are familar with.
- Change the tree as the children notice seasonal changes occuring.

5 — What is the weather like?

Materials and preparation

- days of the week/weather chart

To use a growing weather word vocabulary

To talk about weather observations

Using a weather and 'days of the week' chart is an ideal way to extend children's vocabulary.

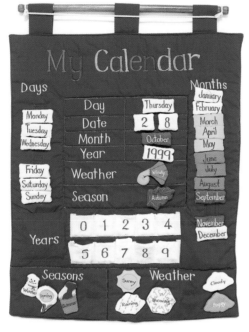

Questions

- What day is it today?
- What is the date?
- What month is it?
- What season is it?
- What is the weather like today?

WHAT TO DO

- Show the children the weather chart and talk about all the elements. Ask the children to describe today's weather and pick the appropriate weather symbols to put on the chart.
- Use the chart on a daily basis to record the date as well as the current weather conditions.

EXTENSION IDEA

- Compare changes in weather conditions between morning and afternoon sessions.

---

6 — Make a weather chart

Materials and preparation

- card • felt-tipped pens • Blu Tac
- sticky backed plastic
make a days of the week chart and laminate it

To use vocabulary to express thoughts with increasing fluency

To recognise changes in the weather

Once children are familiar with days of the week/weather charts, make your own with them.

If you have access to a television, watch a weather forecast with the children.

Questions

- How can we make a picture card to show sunny/rainy weather?
- Has the weather changed today?
- What was the weather like yesterday?
- How many sunny days have we had this week?

WHAT TO DO

- Discuss different kinds of weather with the children and ask them to suggest the kinds of symbol you could make to represent each kind of weather.
- Make the symbols with the children, ensuring that they fit onto the days of the week chart you have made.
- Use the chart and symbols daily to record the weather over the course of one week.
- Discuss with the children how the weather has varied during the week.

Tomorrow's weather

Materials and preparation

• home-made weather map – see Make a weather map (8) below for instructions • picture symbols • Blu Tac to stick the symbols to the weather map • picture and reference books showing a range of weather conditions

 To use a growing vocabulary to convey meaning

 To talk about their observations

To use their imagination through play

This activity will help to develop children's observational skills and extend their descriptive vocabulary about the weather.

TIP Support the role play by extending vocabulary to include language such as showers, temperature.

▶ WHAT TO DO

• Show the children the books and discuss the different kinds of weather. Encourage the children to use descriptive vocabulary.
• Show the children the weather map. Discuss which kind of weather each symbol represents.
• Encourage the children to predict the weather to others, taking fair turns at being weather forecasters and audience members.

EXTENSION IDEA

• Provide large and small pieces of card for children to design and make their own maps and symbols.

👍 Knead the Blu Tac before the activity so that it is pliable and sticks to the symbols easily.

Make a weather map

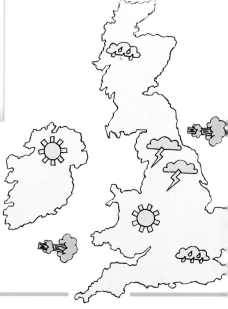

Materials and preparation

• templates from page 63 • scissors • felt-tipped pens • Blu Tac • thin card • sticky-backed plastic
Trace the map template onto pieces of thin card – one for each child
Trace lots of weather symbols onto thin card for the children to cut out

 Can handle scissors with increasing control

 To use a growing vocabulary to convey meaning

 Can talk about their observations

Once children are familiar with weather maps, let them make their own.

1 Look at the maps with the children and talk about what they tell us. Cut out one map for each child.

2 Invite the children to cut out and colour their own weather symbols to use with the maps.

TIP Include vocabulary such as country, island, sea, land, area, coast, inland.

 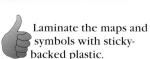 Laminate the maps and symbols with sticky-backed plastic.

42

Our weather centre

Materials and preparation

Resources for recording outdoor weather conditions such as:
a windmill • thermometer • rain gauge
Convert the home corner into a class weather centre, including resources such as: junk television set • maps • pictorial weather symbols • old cameras • binoculars • books • pictures • dressing-up clothes

 To talk about observations

 To observe through imaginative play

 To co-operate with others

 TIP If possible, set up the class weather centre near a window so that children can observe current weather conditions first hand.

The best way to encourage children's interest in the weather is to go outside and observe it with them.

 Make sure children wear appropriate clothes for outdoors.

 Before making any excursion from the nursery, obtain the consent of carers.

▶ WHAT TO DO

- Begin by setting up a real weather centre outdoors, using the resources suggested, to help record the daily weather conditions.
- Discuss setting up a classroom weather centre and ask the children for their suggestions as to what it should contain.
- Encourage turn taking in role play as weather forecasters, camera operators, and audience members.

EXTENSION IDEAS

- Children could design and make artefacts for the weather centre from junk materials.
- Chalk around puddles after the rain to observe the evaporation rate.
- Paint weather pictures.

What shall I wear today?

Materials and preparation

Dressing up clothes to suit a range of weather conditions such as:
rain coat • wellington boots • sun hat • sun dress • shorts • thick jumper • gloves

 To take part in role play with confidence

To talk about the effects of the weather

To demonstrate independence in dressing

This activity can be used as a follow on to Our weather centre (9) page 43.

▶ WHAT TO DO

- Place the clothes in the weather centre and encourage the children to dress up according to the current weather forecaster's predictions.

Questions

- What is the weather forecast?
- What do you think we should wear?
- Will this keep us cool/dry/warm?
- Do we need sunglasses?
- Should I wear a sun hat?

TIME AND MY FOOD

This chapter focuses on the effects time can have on the condition of our food. There are activities for observing change through cooking food for set times, as well as activities involving freezing over time and its effect on liquids. Food decay through exposure to the air over time is also explored through practical investigations. Sensory explorations are encouraged and children are made aware of the important health and safety issues involved and the need to take responsibility for their own personal hygiene. Do remember to inform carers of the ingredients being used if you are going to present any activities that involve tasting, in case of any allergies or particular dietary preferences or restrictions.

Activities in this chapter

1
Mealtimes
A practical activity involving children talking about their usual daily mealtimes and sequencing them

2
Sequencing a meal
Make sequencing cards based on meals from a range of different cultures

3
Preparing a meal
Following the stages involved in the preparation of a meal from looking at the recipe through to doing the washing up!

4
Making toast
A practical activity involving the use of a timer to observe the changes to slices of bread as they are toasted

5
Cooking with eggs
Investigating the differences between raw eggs and the effects of cooking them over time

6
What is inside my apple?
Exploring a familiar fruit using all the senses

7
Changing apples
An extension activity to find out what happens to an apple after it has been cut open and left exposed to the air over time

8
Bananas
Finding out about the ripening process using a familiar fruit

9
Making ice lollies
Investigating the effects on liquids of freezing over time

10
What is in the water tray?
A practical activity to investigate what happens to ice when it is exposed to warmer conditions over time

11
Wobbly jelly
Making jellies to experience dissolving in heat and setting in cold conditions over time

1   Mealtimes

Materials and preparation
- range of meals that children would typically eat • some fruit • some cups

 To talk about their experiences

 To talk about family events

 To use mathematical language

 To express own feelings

In this activity, children are encouraged to think about when they eat particular foods.

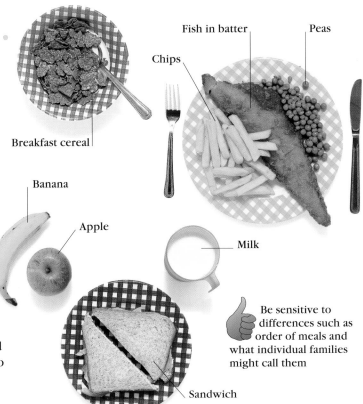

Breakfast cereal

Chips

Fish in batter

Peas

Banana

Apple

Milk

Be sensitive to differences such as order of meals and what individual families might call them

Sandwich

TIP You could cut out pictures of meals and drinks from magazines to stick onto paper plates, dishes and cups.

▶ WHAT TO DO
- Talk about our daily meals and let the children tell you about their favourite foods.
- Look at the meals and encourage the children to sequence them in order of when they might eat them.
- Introduce mealtime words, such as breakfast, snack, lunch, dinner, supper, dessert, pudding, sweet, cutlery, knife fork, spoon, and use ordinal number language.

Questions
- Which meal would you eat first?
- What would you eat at lunchtime?
- Which food would you eat last?
- Which is your favourite?

---

2   Sequencing a meal

Materials and preparation
- pictures of food from different cultures cut out of magazines showing a range of courses • card • glue

 To develop respect for cultural differences

 To talk about their observations

 To sort, order and sequence things

You will need pictures of a range of dishes for this activity.

Label any unusual dishes on the backs of the cards.

▶ WHAT TO DO
- Make sets of mealtime cards typical of a variety of cultures, such as Italian and Indian dishes. Include starters, main courses and desserts in each set.
- Talk about the different foods and encourage the children to sort the cards and order them.

TIP Involve families from a variety of cultures by asking them for suggestions.
- Invite members of families from a variety of cultures to come in to talk the children about their foods and mealtimes.

EXTENSION IDEA
Make ordinal number cards for children to place by their sequences.

The activities on these two pages show you how to develop children's sense of time by preparing and eating a meal together.

Materials and preparation

recipe book · paper · pencils · money

 To become aware of features of the local area

 To handle books with care and know the words carry meaning
To use pictures and symbols to communicate meaning

 To develop mathematical understanding to solve a practical problem

 Explain safe hygiene practices to the children, and ensure that you are aware of any special diets.

(Recipe book shown: Little cheese tarts — steps 1 to 8)

Shopping list: 150g plain flour / 75g margarine / salt / small tin of sweetcorn / 50g cheese / 1 egg / 3 tablespoons milk

1 Look at and talk about the recipe book, identifying the meal you want to make.

2 Encourage the children to write shopping lists of the ingredients they need to prepare the meal.

Materials and preparation

potatoes · potato peeler · saucepan of water · hob · milk · butter · potato masher

Choose which meal elements you will prepare with the children – we have chosen mashed potatoes. The nursery staff can prepare the remainder.

WHAT TO DO

- Tell the children that they are going to work together to prepare a meal.
- Follow steps one to ten for instructions on how to carry out the activity.
- Include vocabulary such as recipe, ingredients, shopping list, cost, price, change.

Questions

- What shall we make?
- What do we need?
- Where can we get it from?
- How can we get it?
- Where is the nearest shop?

EXTENSION IDEA

- If your nursery is near a shop, take the children out with you to experience selecting and paying for their ingredients. Ensure you request permission from carers before taking the children out and always have a high adult to child ratio.

3 Investigate the potatoes for colour and feel, and peel them as the children watch. Talk about how other vegetables are prepared.

4 Boil the potatoes, making children aware of the health and safety issues, and talk about the length of time needed to cook them.

5 Drain the cooked potatoes and let the children watch as you mash them, adding the milk and butter.

Materials and preparation

plates · cutlery · cups · jug of drink
prepared meal · table · chairs

 To handle cutlery with increasing control

 To demonstrate independence in personal hygiene.
To behave appropriately

 To count using objects, matching sets of objects to one 'place', and to understand mathematical language

Once the potatoes are mashed, take them into the kitchen ready to be served with the rest of the food.

- Ask the children to set the table. Give each child specific tasks, such as collecting the juice, placing the cutlery on the table and so on.
- Introduce appropriate language, such as full, empty, one, two, and so on, as the children perform each task.

6 Ask the children to lay the table, counting how many items are needed for one of everything per child. Use positional language as they lay out the cutlery.

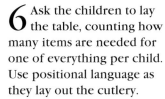

7 Let them count out the number of cups, pour out the drinks, and place them on the table.

8 Ask the children how many meals need to be served. Serve the food and let the children carry each plate to the table.

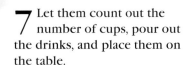

9 Encourage the children to talk about the various textures and tastes of the food.

10 Ask the children to help you clear away and wash up the plates afterwards.

Making toast

Use this activity to show children how the appearance of bread can alter in stages.

 To be willing to explore new learning

 To talk about similarities, differences, and change

 Put up a notice informing carers of the ingredients in case of any allergies.
Ensure the children are aware of the dangers of electricity and of safe practices.

▶ WHAT TO DO

· Investigate one slice of bread, noticing colour, smell and texture.
· Set the toaster to a low setting, toast one slice and observe the results
· Set the toaster to a higher setting, toast another slice. Compare the bread and toast.
· Let the children taste the bread and toast to compare the differences.

Questions

· What changes can you see?
· Which piece is the lightest/darkest colour?
· Which piece did we toast for the longest time?
· Which one did you like best when you tasted it?

 Fresh, sliced bread

 Toasted bread

Burnt bread

EXTENSION IDEAS

· Develop children's understanding of fractions by cutting the toast into halves and quarters.

Cooking with eggs

In this activity, children develop their counting ability and comparative skills.

 To count and take away through practical activities

 To ask questions to gain information

 Partially cooked or raw egg can be dangerous for young children. Ensure thorough cooking and do not allow them to touch the raw egg.

 Put up a notice informing carers of the ingredients in case of any allergies.

 Ensure that the children are aware of safety issues when you are cooking.

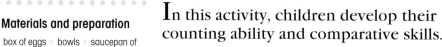

1 Count the eggs and take one out of the box.

2 Talk about the egg. Crack it into the bowl to observe the contents.

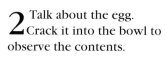

3 Boil the egg. Leave to cool then investigate the contents. Compare the differences. Take another egg and scramble it. Discuss how the texture has changed during cooking.

Questions

· How many eggs are there?
· How many are left now we have taken one out?
· What is inside?
· What colour do you think it will be?
· Does the shell look different now it is cooked?
· Do you think it will be the same inside when we crack it open?

EXTENSION IDEAS

· Try other ways of cooking with eggs such as frying or poaching.
· If you have access to fertilised eggs and an incubator you could observe hatching and growth.

What is inside my apple?

Look at whole and halved apples to develop children's vocabulary and comparative skills.

Materials and preparation

apples • a blunt knife • paper plates or serviettes • magnifying glasses

 To explore and recognise similarities and differences

 To respond to sensory experiences

 To develop mathematical language of fractions, counting and shapes

EXTENSION IDEAS

- Count, compare and record the number of pips in each apple.
- Plant the pips to observe growth over time.
- Make close observational drawings.
- Use one or two apples to make prints with paint.
- Cook some apples to eat.

Apple core

Apple pip

TIP Inform carers of the purpose of the activity and request donations of apples.

WHAT TO DO

- Invite each child to choose an apple to examine and describe using their senses of touch, sight, and smell.
- Help them to cut their apples into halves, and then investigate the insides using the magnifying glasses. What are they like now?
- Invite each child to bite into one half of their apple to explore the taste. Can they hear any sounds?
- Extend vocabulary by supplying words such as peel, core, stalk.

Questions

- Pose open questions such as 'What do you think it will be like inside?'

Changing apples

This activity can be used as a follow on to What is inside my apple? (6) page 49.

Materials and preparation

apple halves • magnifying glasses • lemon juice • pictorial sign reminding children not to touch the decaying apples

 To use a growing vocabulary to express thoughts

 To observe changes to an apple over time

 To demonstrate independence in personal hygiene

EXTENSION IDEA

Set up other food decay experiments for the children to observe.

1 Sprinkle lemon juice on one set of apple halves to maintain the colour. This will enable the children to compare colour differences with older apple halves.

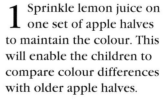

2 Leave one set of apple halves out to turn brown. Encourage the children to observe them at half-hourly intervals.

WHAT TO DO

- Encourage children to observe changes to the apples over time, stressing the importance of not touching them for health and safety reasons.
- Talk about healthy eating: why we should always wash our hands before eating to avoid the spread of germs, and how we can protect our teeth from tooth decay.

Questions

- What has happened?
- What differences/ changes can you see?
- Would this be good to eat now? Why not?

Bananas

Materials and preparation

3 bananas:
- one under ripe
- one ready to eat
- one over ripe

 To demonstrate independence in personal hygiene

 To observe changes over time

 To use a growing vocabulary to express thoughts

 Let the children observe the green banana ripening over time.

Buy bananas over several days for this activity to ensure you have three bananas in very different stages of ripeness.

Green under ripe banana

Yellow ripe banana

Black over ripe banana

▶ WHAT TO DO

- Show the children the bananas. Encourage them to look at the differences in colour and feel the differences by pressing fingers into the unpeeled bananas.

Questions

- What colour is it?
- How does it feel?
- What happens if you try to push your fingers into it?
- Which do you think is the oldest/youngest?
- What colour do you think it will be inside?
- Which do you think would be the best to eat?

Making ice lollies

Materials and preparation

jugs of water • squash or juice in different flavours • ice cube trays or lolly moulds • clean lolly sticks • spoons
Write each child's name on a clean lolly stick

 To ask questions to gain information

 To recognise own name

 To respond to sensory experiences

 To solve a simple practical problem

 Inform carers of the purpose of the activity and of the ingredients being used in case of any allergies.

This activity will be very popular on a warm summer's day!

Questions

- What can we do to this to make it change into an ice lolly?
- What has happened?
- How will we know whose is whose?
- How will we get the ice lollies out?
- What does it taste like?

▶ WHAT TO DO

- Talk about the liquids and ask each child which flavour lolly they would like to make
- Help them pour some liquid into a mould and find their own lolly stick to put in it.
- Put the lollies in the freezer. When frozen, let the children find their labelled lolly and let them eat them.

What's in the water tray?

Materials and preparation
- ice tray • food colouring
- small objects that will fit in the ice tray • jug of water
- plate to turn ice cubes out on to

 To look closely at changes

 To express own ideas

 To respond through sense of touch

To explore new learning

Prepare the ice cubes at the beginning of the session and observe the frozen ice cubes at the end to help children gain a sense of how long it takes to freeze an ice cube.

Put the ice cubes in a bowl to contain the melting water.

EXTENSION IDEA
Put frozen blocks of ice in the water tray as icebergs, along with boats.

✚ Supervise children closely to ensure they do not eat the small objects inside the ice cubes.

▶ WHAT TO DO

- Show the children the ice tray, food colouring, small items and water. Ask them to help you decide which colour ice cubes to make and which items to freeze inside the cubes.
- Encourage the children to feel and describe the ice blocks, telling you of any changes they observe.

Questions
- What do you think they are made of?
- Are they keeping their shapes?
- What is happening? Why?
- What colour is the water now?
- What could we do to make it solid again?

Wobbly jelly

Materials and preparation
- tablets of jelly in different flavours
- a different shaped mould for each group • hot water
- bowls • spoons

 To explore change

 To use an increasing vocabulary to express thoughts

 To demonstrate independence in personal hygiene

Ensure you are aware of any allergies before carrying out this activity.

✚ Emphasise safety issues when handling boiling water.

▶ WHAT TO DO

- Let the children feel and describe the jelly using their senses of sight, smell and touch, as they tear the cubes into the bowl.
- Carefully pour boiling water over the jelly cubes and ask the children to observe and describe the changes.
- Add cold water and pour the mixture into the mould. Leave to set.
- Share the set jelly with the children, discussing the texture, colour, and taste.

Questions
Extend the children's vocabulary by including language such as dissolve, set, mould, shape, stretchy, solid, liquid.
- How does it look/feel/ smell?
- What is happening/has happened? Why?

TIME AND GROWTH

This chapter contains a range of activities intended to develop children's understanding of the effects of time on some alternative life forms in the natural world, including plants, butterflies, and frogs. They learn about growth, change and life cycles through close observation. There are opportunities for both outdoor and indoor investigations, and for recording; the need for care and concern for plants and creatures in the natural environment is also emphasised. Children are made aware of conservation issues and of their responsibility for the preservation and condition of our environment. The relevant health and safety issues are also highlighted.

Activities in this chapter

1
How do plants grow?
An opportunity to examine the growth of a bean over time through close observation

2
My bean diary
An extension activity involving children in recording their observations of the stages in bean growth over time

3
What do plants need?
Identifying the best conditions to ensure plant growth over time through a fair test

4
Cress sandwiches
An extension activity harvesting the fully grown cress and making sandwiches to share

5
Absorbing water
A practical activity enabling children to observe how plants absorb water through osmosis over time

6
What else can I grow?
Design and make plant pots to grow seeds in for planting out in the nursery grounds or in tubs

7
Let's design a garden
Creating miniature gardens to encourage plant care using natural resources and small world models

8
A real garden
Creating a class garden plot in the nursery grounds stocked with plants and vegetables for the children to maintain

9
Living things outside
Exploring the outdoor environment as nature detectives to discover other living things, and to consider conservation issues

10
From caterpillar to ...
Finding out about the stages in the life cycle of a butterfly

11
The Hungry Caterpillar
Reinforcing the life cycle of a butterfly through retelling a familiar story and recording part of it

12
How do frogs grow?
Investigating the stages in the life cycle of a frog through close observation

13
Five little speckled frogs
An extension activity involving learning a song and adding percussion accompaniment

1   How do plants grow?

Materials and preparation

- glass jars • one bean for each child
- sticky labels • pencils • blotting paper
- sand • water

 To look closely at change and record observations

 To recognise/write own name

 To use comparative measurement language

 To demonstrate care for growing things

 Encourage comparative language such as taller/shorter.

Broad beans are quick and easy to grow, making them ideal for children to observe and record their development.

 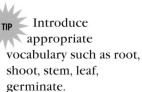 

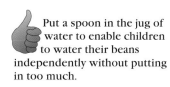 **TIP** Introduce appropriate vocabulary such as root, shoot, stem, leaf, germinate.

Put a spoon in the jug of water to enable children to water their beans independently without putting in too much.

▶ WHAT TO DO

- Look at and talk about the beans
- Ask each child to try to write their own name on a label and stick it on a jar
- Help them to roll the blotting paper into cylinders and to place it in the jars. Spoon sand into the centre of each jar.
- Let the children plant one bean between the blotting paper and the glass
- Explain that they will be responsible for caring for and watering their own beans.
- Water the beans regularly.

---

2   My bean diary

Materials and preparation

- homemade books • pencils
- beans in jars • magnifying glasses

 To observe change and record own observations

 To use pictures and symbols to convey meaning

This activity can be used as a follow on to How do plants grow? (2) page 53.

TIP Take photographs of the beans at each stage of their growth to form a record.

- Encourage the children to compare the different growth rates of their beans.

EXTENSION IDEAS

- Make bean growth collage pictures using real beans, white wool for roots and green paper for stalks and leaves.
- Repeat the activity in spring or summer to grow sweet peas or sunflowers for the garden plot.

▶ WHAT TO DO

- Explain to the children that they are going to be making their own books to show how their beans grow.
- Ask them to draw a picture of their newly planted beans on the first page.
- As key growth stages are observed, ask children to use their books to draw what they can see.
- They could also attempt their own writing or you could scribe for them.

Questions

- Which way is the root growing?
- Which way is the shoot growing?
- How long did it take to germinate?
- Why is it growing?
- What do you think it will grow into?

What do plants need?

Materials and preparation

- two small, clean plastic trays • cotton wool • cress seeds
- water • two small, clean plastic lids • labels • pipe cleaner

To talk about what plants need for healthy growth

To use a growing vocabulary

To show care and concern for living things

You can use cress or mustard seeds or both for this activity.

1 Line two trays with cotton wool. Soak the cotton wool in one tray.

2 Sprinkle cress seeds on to the cotton wool in both trays.

3 Cover one tray with the lid and leave both trays in a warm place to germinate.

EXTENSION IDEAS

- Share the story 'The Tiny Seed' by Eric Carle, published by Puffin.
- Grow cress in eggshell halves and decorate them to make Humpty Dumptys.

TIPS Pose open questions to stimulate inquiry and reasoning each time you observe the trays.
- You could use mustard seeds instead of cress seeds.

WHAT TO DO

- Sow the seeds with the children and then ask what they think the seeds will need to make them grow.

Cress seeds will not grow at all without water.

Cress seeds need water and light to grow properly.

Cress sandwiches

Materials and preparation

- sliced bread • butter • blunt knife • cress • paper plates • napkins

To handle a blunt knife safely and with care

To name squares, rectangles, triangles, fractions, halves and quarters

To share with others

This activity reinforces mathematical language such as quantity and shape.

Questions

- Are there enough for you to have one each?
- How many pieces must we cut the sandwich into for you to have one each?

WHAT TO DO

- Let the children carefully spread butter on two slices of bread with the blunt knife.
- Ask them to sprinkle the cress on one slice of bread and to place the second slice on top of it.
- Cut and share the sandwich equally between all four children.

Inform carers of the ingredients in case of any allergies.

Remind the children to wash their hands before beginning this activity.

5 — Absorbing water

Materials and preparation
- water • glasses • blue food colouring • celery sticks with leaves

 To talk about their observations

 To use vocabulary to convey own thoughts

Set up this activity before the session, so the children can see the change by the end.

Celery sticks that have just been put in coloured water will still be green.

By the end of the session, the leaf tips of the celery will be blue.

TIP Put one piece of celery in a glass of clear water to remind the children of the colour of the celery stick before it absorbs blue food dye.

▶ WHAT TO DO

- Talk about what plants need to grow. Mix some food colouring into a glass of water. Put the celery stick into the glass. Ask the children to tell you about any changes they notice as the plants absorb the liquid.

Questions

- How can we make this water look blue?
- What has happened to the celery?
- Why do you think it has happened?

---

6 — What else can I grow?

Materials and preparation
- clean yoghurt pots • paper • glue • felt tips • scissors • sticky labels • soil • seeds

 To select and use tools and materials to decortate pots

 To listen and respond to the rhyme
To read/write own name on the label

 To work independently

This activity enables each child to be responsible for the care of their own plants.

Mary, Mary

Mary, Mary, quite contrary,

How does your garden grow?

With sliver bells and cockle shells,

And pretty maids all in a row!

TIP Some children could write own name labels to stick on the pots.

▶ WHAT TO DO

- Say the rhyme 'Mary, Mary Quite Contrary' together.
- Invite the children to design and decorate a yoghurt pot to grow some seeds in.
- Plant seeds in the labelled pots.

Use easy-to-grow seeds such as nasturtiums, sweet peas and sunflowers.

Provide magnifying glasses for close observation of the seeds.

Questions

- What do you think you will need?
- How can you make it stick on?
- Does it work?

Let's design a garden

Materials and preparation

- selection of junk materials • powder paints • paint brushes • pictures of different kinds of garden for the children to refer to

 To select own materials and use skills learned

 To handle appropriate tools safely

Encourge children to think about space and position by designing junk gardens.

Materials and preparation

- bowls • shards of clay or stones • soil
- small pots • seeds • small plants • small world models • gravel • shells

 To follow a plan to create a garden

 To work imaginatively with new materials

 To handle appropriate tools safely

 To work purposefully alongside other children

Now let the children turn their models into real miniature gardens!

▶ WHAT TO DO

- Place all the materials on the table. Talk to the children about different kinds of garden and invite them to make their ideal garden out of the materials.

Questions

- Ask what they plan to put in different areas of their garden and talk about safety issues if, for example, they want to put things in a pond.

▶ WHAT TO DO

- Once the children have designed their gardens with the junk materials, invite them to recreate the gardens with real plants and soil.
- You could make the garden shown here to inspire and encourage the children.

TIP Ask parents and carers to donate old washing up bowls and small pots, so the children have a range of shapes with which to design their gardens.

1 Put clay shards or small stones in the base of the bowl for drainage.

2 Put in the soil, and a plastic pot if a pond is required. Sow some seeds and add plants.

3 Water regularly. Add gravel pathways and small world people and animals.

8 — A real garden

Materials and preparation
- gardening tools • wheelbarrow
- plants

 To talk about features of the outdoor environment

 To use tools safely

 To treat living things with care

 Keep a rota so that all children take turns to check growth and water the plants.

If you do not have a garden, supply large tubs in which the children can nurture and tend garden plants.

 Talk about which plants flower at particular times of year.

▶ WHAT TO DO

- Let the children help to dig and prepare the garden plot.
- Plant out some of the things you have been growing in the classroom, such as seedlings.
- Plant a range of seeds and bulbs that grow at different times of year.
- Extend the children's vocabulary by introducing appropriate language such as seeds, plants, flowers, vegetables, weeds, buds.

✚ Remind children to always wash their hands after gardening.

9 — Living things outside

Materials and preparation
- magnifying glasses • collection pots with a lining of soft grass

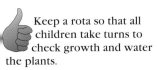 To explore the natural environment outside
To recognise features of living things around them

 To treat living things with concern
To show feelings

Questions
- Ask the children to name different categories such as insects, spiders, birds and so on.
- Encourage children to describe colour, size movement, shape, and other characteristics and any sounds they hear.

 Ensure all children wash their hands back in the nursery.

Take the children out on a nature detective hunt to look for minibeasts and other living things.

TIP Make sure any minibeasts you collect are safely returned to their habitat
- If you are taking children out, remember to get permission from carers first, and ensure adequate levels of supervision.

▶ WHAT TO DO

- Ask the children to use quiet voices and to move carefully to avoid disturbing any wildlife and encourage them to look carefully under stones and logs, and up in corners.

EXTENSION IDEAS
- Discuss conservation issues such as not disturbing birds' nests picking wild flowers in the spring, or littering.

From caterpillar to...

Materials and preparation

- share stories such as 'The Hungry Caterpillar' by Eric Carle, and 'Caterpillar, Caterpillar' by Vivian French
- life cycle puzzles, pictures and non-fiction books

 To observe and talk about change

 To show feelings in response to experiences

TIP Introduce appropriate language such as egg, caterpillar, chrysalis, cocoon, pupa, butterfly, symmetrical patterns, proboscis, nectar.

The transformation of a caterpillar into a butterfly is a magical process that will hold the attention of all children.

1 This brightly coloured caterpillar will soon metamorphose into a butterfly.

2 The caterpillar is now enveloped inside the cocoon.

3 The caterpillar is turning into a butterfly inside the cocoon.

4 The caterpillar has turned into a butterfly and is emerging from the cocoon.

5 This brightly coloured butterfly is called a monarch.

▶ WHAT TO DO

- Use the books and pictures to track the development from egg to butterfly.
- Contact your local wildlife organisation and arrange for a caterpillar to be donated to the nursery so that the children can observe its metamorphosis themselves.

The Hungry Caterpillar

Materials and preparation

- paper • pencils • crayons

 To be aware of the stages in the life cycle of the butterfly

 To use pictures and writing to retell the story

 To handle pencils and crayons with increasing control

 To recognise numbers 1-5 and to sequence cards with objects depicted

Have a Hungry Caterpillar feast, involving tasting little bits of the food the caterpillar ate, first informing carers in case of any allergies.

This activity develops mathematical language by sorting pages from 'The Hungry Caterpillar' by Eric Carle. Puffin.

▶ WHAT TO DO

- Read the story with the children ensuring they are familiar with the sequence of events.
- Make sequencing cards showing the fruits the hungry caterpillar ate for ordering from 1-5. Ask the children to order them.
- Discuss the children's knowledge of what caterpillars really eat.

EXTENSION IDEA

- Make zigzag books for children to record the sequence of the story in their own pictures and writing.

How do frogs grow?

Materials and preparation
- tank of pond water with some frog-spawn, pond weed and stones
- magnifying glasses

 To look closely at change

 To respond to the experience with wonder

Take the children to a local pond to collect frog-spawn in the spring for this activity. Ensure a high adult:child ratio for safety.

1 Frogs lay large blobs of frog-spawn in ponds every spring.

2 Frog-spawn quickly develop into tadpoles and feed on plant life.

3 Within days, tadpoles start growing legs and turning into frogs.

4 Once fully developed, frogs leave the water and live on land.

EXTENSION IDEAS
- Make collage frog-spawn using net, bubble wrap and black paint glued onto pond shapes.

▶ WHAT TO DO
- Get the children to observe regularly the tank and to talk about what they notice.

TIP Introduce appropriate language such as frog-spawn, jelly, tadpoles, tails, wriggle, front legs, back legs, froglets and amphibian.
- Release the froglets back into their natural habitat when their back legs have developed.

13

Catching fish

 To sing and use some instruments

To count to ten using rhyme

To work together with others

Extend children's awareness of pond life and singing this fish rhyme.

Five Little Speckled Frogs

One, two, three, four, five, *(Count on fingers)*

Once I caught a fish alive; *(Wriggle hand like a fish)*

Six, seven, eight, nine, ten, *(Count fingers)*

Then I let him go again. *(Pretend to throw fish back)*

Why did you let him go?

Because he bit my finger so! *(Shake hand violently)*

Which finger did he bite?

This little finger on the right! *(Hold up little finger of right hand)*

▶ WHAT TO DO
- Teach the children the song, and actions to it.
- Introduce a range of percussion instruments.
- Ask the children to describe the sounds each instrument makes.

TIP Leave the instruments and resources out as an independent choice activity.
- Make shakers from junk materials.

Questions
- Which instrument would make a good sound for the fish splashing back in the water?
- Can a fish really bite you?

Resources

This section contains suggestions for a useful range of material to supplement the activities in this book. The booklist below contains a selection of fiction books that include stories, poems, rhymes and songs, as well as some suggestions for non-fiction books, which provide information. You will find templates to support some activities on pages 62-63. The index on page 64 lists every activity contained in **All About Time**.

STORY BOOKS

'Avocado baby', John Burningham. Red Fox.

'Ben's Birthday Party', Rosemary Border. MacDonald Out & About.

'Can't You Sleep Little Bear?', Martin Waddell and Barbara Firth. Walker Books

'Caterpillar, Caterpillar', Vivian French. Walker Books.

'Dad, I Can't Sleep', Michael Foreman. Andersen Press.

'Dogger', Shirley Hughes. Bodley Head.

'Elmer', David McKee. Andersen Press.

'Gran and Grandpa', Helen Oxenbury. Walker books.

'Grandpa', John Burningham. Puffin.

'Granny is a Darling', Kady MacDonald Denton. Walker Books.

'Handa's Surprise', Eileen Browne. Walker Books.

'In the Middle of the Night', Kathy Henderson. Walker Books.

'It's My Birthday', Helen Oxenbury. Walker books.

'Jack and the Beanstalk'. Ladybird books.

'Jasper's Beanstalk', Butterworth and Inkpen. Hodder and Stoughton.

'Jenny's Baby Sister', Peter Smith. Picture Lions.

'Jim and the Beanstalk', Raymond Briggs. Puffin.

'Just Like Me', Jan Ormerod. Walker books.

'Mog and the Dark', Judith Kerr. Collins.

'Mrs Mopple's Washing Line', Anita Hewett. Picture Puffins.

'My Brother Sean', Petronella Breinberg. Red Fox.

'My Naughty Little Sister', Dorothy Edwards. Methuen.

'Old Bear', Jane Hissey. Red Fox.

'On Friday Something Funny Happened', John Prater. Picture Puffins.

'Once There Were Giants', Martin Waddell. Walker Books.

'One Smiling Grandma', Anne Marie Linden. Mammoth.

'Peace at Last', Jill Murphy. MacMillan.

'Pumpkin, Pumpkin', Jeanne Titherington. Julia MacRae Books.

'Something Special', Nicola Moon. Orchard Books.

'Sophie and the New Baby', Catherine Anholt. Orchard Books.

'Tell Me Something Happy Before I Go To Sleep', Joyce Dunbar and Debi Gliori. Doubleday.

'Ten, Nine, Eight', Molly Bang. Picture Puffins.

'The Baby Who Wouldn't Go To Bed', Helen Cooper. Picture Corgi.

'The Green Banana Hunt', Jenny Bent. Scholastic.

'The Little Red Hen'. Ladybird books.

'The Lonely Only Mouse', Wendy Smith. Puffin.

'The Patchwork Cat', Nicola Bayley and William Mayne. Jonathan Cape.

'The Tiny Seed', Eric Carle. Puffin.

'The Very Busy Spider', Eric Carle. Hamish Hamilton.

Resources

'The Very Hungry Caterpillar', Eric Carle. Hamish Hamilton.

'Titch', Pat Hutchings. Picture Puffins.

'What Will the Weather Be Like Today?', Paul Kazuko Roagers. Orchard books.

'When Willy Went to the Wedding', Judith Kerr. Picture Lions.

'You'll Soon Grow into Them Titch', Pat Hutchings. Red Fox.

INFORMATION BOOKS

'Autumn', Fiona Pragoff. Victor Gollancz.

'Find Out About the Weather', Terry Jennings. BBC.

'I Wonder Why the Sun Rises', Brenda Walpole. Kingfisher.

'Jobs People Do', Christopher Maynard. Dorling Kindersley.

'My Book of Time', Anthony Lewis. Leopard.

'My First Book of Time', Claire Llewellyn. Dorling Kindersley.

'My First Look at the Seasons', Dorling Kindersley.

'Rainy Day', Mick Manning. Franklin Watts.

'Seasons', Brian Wildsmith. Oxford University Press.

'Sleeping', Joy Richardson. Hodder & Stoughton.

'Spring', Fiona Pragoff. Victor Gollancz.

'Summer', Fiona Pragoff. Victor Gollancz.

'The Sun', David Glover. Ginn Science.

'The Wind', David Glover. Ginn Science.

'What's the Time?', Tony Bradman. Cambridge University Press.

'What's the Time?', Richard and Nicky Halls. Cherrytree.

'Winter', Fiona Pragoff. Victor Gollancz.

SONGS, POEMS AND RHYMES

'Five Speckled Frogs' and 'The Rainbow Song' are from Apusskidu. A&C Black.

'Fruits', Valerie Bloom. MacMillan.

'Happiness: John Had Great Big Waterproof Boots On' can be found in 'When We Were Very Young', A.A. Milne. Magnet Books.

'Jelly on the Plate'

'The Ladybird Book of Rhymes', Dorothy and John Taylor. Ladybird Books.

'The Sun Has Got His Hat On', Noel Coward.

'Twinkle, Twinkle, Little Star' is included in 'High, Low', Dolly Pepper. A&C Black.

The following can be found in 'The Tinderbox Song Book'. A&C Black.

'Helping Grandma Jones'

'How Do You Feel?'

'I've Got a Body'

'I Went to the Cabbages'

'Let It Be'

'One, Two, Three, Slowly Walks My Grandad'

'One Year Older'

'Song of the Clock'

'The Tidy Song'

'Weather Song'

'Who Has Seen the Wind?'

The following can be found in 'This Little Puffin…', Elizabeth Matterson. Puffin Books:

'Here We Go Round the Mulberry Bush'

'I Hear Thunder'

'Incy Wincy Spider'

The following can be found in 'Mother Goose, A Collection of Nursery Rhymes', Brian Wildsmith. Oxford University Press:

'Boys and Girls Come Out to Play'

'Bye Baby Bunting'

'Hicketty, Picketty My Black Hen'

'Hickory, Dickory Dock'

'Humpty Dumpty'

'Hush a Bye Baby'

'Mary, Mary, Quite Contrary'

'Monday's Child is Fair of Face'

'Solomon Grundy'

'Thirty Days Hath September'

'Wee Willie Winkie'

Templates

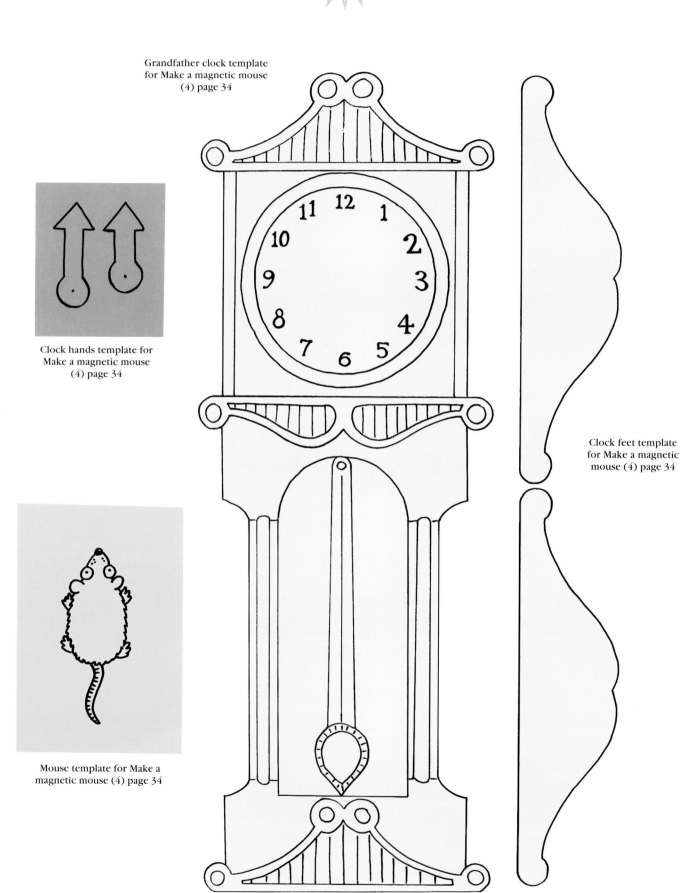

Grandfather clock template
for Make a magnetic mouse
(4) page 34

Clock hands template for
Make a magnetic mouse
(4) page 34

Clock feet template
for Make a magnetic
mouse (4) page 34

Mouse template for Make a
magnetic mouse (4) page 34

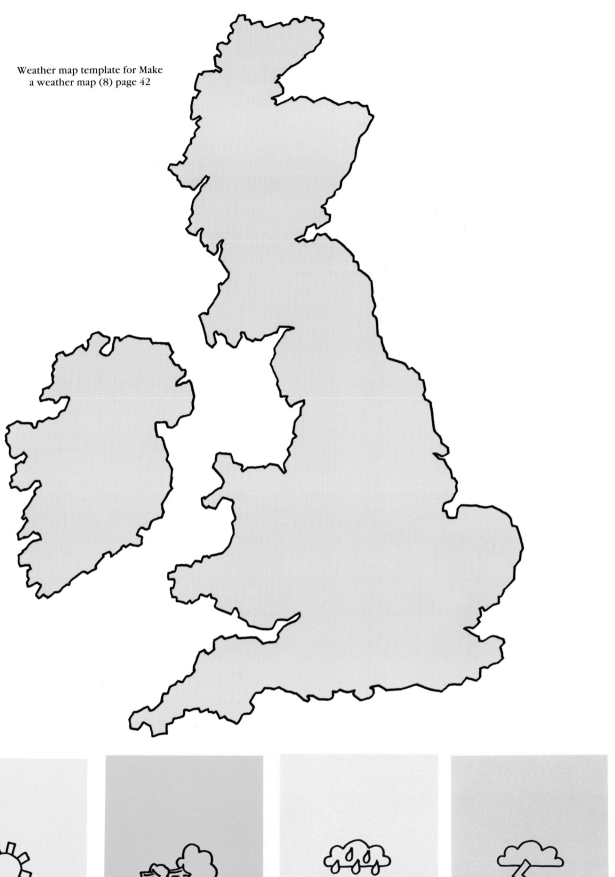

Weather map template for Make
a weather map (8) page 42

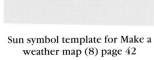

Sun symbol template for Make a
weather map (8) page 42

Wind symbol template for Make a
weather map (8) page 42

Rain symbol template for Make a
weather map (8) page 42

Storm symbol template for Make a
weather map (8) page 42

Index

Acknowledgments

Nursery World would like to thank:

Hope Education for providing many of the props used in this book; Jim Copley for props and templates; Alternative View Studios and Colin Bunner for digital music; Denise Blake for picture research.

Picture credits:

T top; B bottom; C centre; L left; R right;

Scott Camazine/Oxford Scientific Films: 58 TLC
Ken Cole/Natural Science Photos: 58 TRC
Michael Fogden/Oxford Scientific Films: 58 TL
HL Fox/Oxford Scientific Films: 57 BR
Pam Hickman/Natural Science Photos: 58 TCL

John Mitchell/Oxford Scientific Films: 58 TCR
Richard Revels/Naural Science Photos: 59 TR
I West/Natural Science Photos: 59 TL
David Yendall/Natural Science Photos: 59 CL, CR

Every effort has been made to trace the copyright holders. Times Supplements Limited apologises for any unintentional omissions and would be pleased, in such cases, to add an acknowledgment in future editions.